A Month of Sundays

"No other modern public speaker does what the preacher tries to do. The trial attorney has glossy photographs and bagged evidence to hand around; the teacher has blackboards and overhead projectors; the politician has brass bands and media consultants. All the preacher has is words."
—*Barbara Brown Taylor,* The Preaching Life,
  Cowley Publications, 1993, p. 79

"The minister has a job cut from monumental dimensions. The specifications for rehabilitating a usable imaginable worshipful vision of reality . . . thrust a person beyond all normal limits of human resources. The minister must probe the past till he/she finds the quick of it and knows beyond . . . a doubt the broad and everlasting realities in it which run like a living stream into our own day. The minister must probe the present and suffer the full brunt of its tumultuous power and passion, separating with painful threshing the wheat from the chaff of his/her own mind and heart. The minister must take the Bible, a very old book fashioned in archaic languages and forms, and unveil the present intimacy of its radical realities. The minister must handle the mixed and perplexing chaos of mortal circumstance, the old and the new, the great and the inconsequential, the sacred and the profane, and . . . make sense of things, or be honest and humble in knowing he/she can do no more than face them wisely and bravely. The minister must learn to see the primordial truth in small events, the sublime in common unexpected places, the glory of grace in humble persons, the Son of God in a 'litter of scorn.' Everywhere, the minister must have eyes to see what mortal eyes too often miss, and the intelligence both to look for it and to confirm it when it is found.
—*Samuel H. Miller, "But Find the Point Again," address delivered at Harvard Divinity School convocation, September 30, 1959*

A Month of Sundays

Making Sense of Things

Earle W. Fike Jr.

Foreword by Donald F. Durnbaugh

Herald
Press

Scottdale, Pennsylvania
Waterloo, Ontario

Library of Congress Cataloguing-in-Publication Data
Fike, Earle W., 1930-
  A Month of Sundays : making sense of things / Earle W. Fike, Jr
  p.cm.
  Includes bibliographical references
  ISBN 0-8361-9142-0 (alk. paper)
    1. Church of the Brethren—Sermons. 2. Sermons, American—
    20th century. I. Title

BX8127 .F54 2001
252'.097—dc21

00-050578

A MONTH OF SUNDAYS
Copyright © 2001 by Herald Press, Scottdale, Pa. 15683
      Published simultaneously in Canada by Herald Press,
      Waterloo, Ont. N2L 6H7. All rights reserved
Library of Congress Catalog Number: 00-050578
International Standard Book Number: 0-8361-9142-0
Printed in the United States of America
Book design by Gwen M. Stamm, Herald Press, and Michael A. King,
Pandora Press U.S.; cover design by Gwen M. Stamm

10 09 08 07 06 05 04 03 02 01 00   10 9 8 7 6 5 4 3 2 1

To order or request information, please call
1-800-759-4447 (individuals); 1-800-245-7894 (trade).
Website: www.mph.org

To
Joseph W. and Dove Fike Miller,
uncle and aunt by blood but my parents
by their choice, who in their life and service incarnated
the love of God in simple and generous ways.

Contents

Foreword by Donald F. Durnbaugh   11
Author's Preface   15

Foreword

Known in many Christian circles as an excellent craftsman of compelling sermons, Earle W. Fike Jr. here presents a judicious and delightful sample of texts he has delivered over many years of pastoral ministry. His careful biblical exegesis, clear and direct style, apt choice of vocabulary, and intriguing illustrations are apparent in this wide-ranging anthology.

Loosely organized into four sections, the thirty-two selections hold the reader's interest, just as they did the attention of those originally graced by the messages. I have heard many of his sermons as his colleague on a seminary faculty, as auditor in denominational convocations, and especially as a member of the Stone Church of the Brethren, Huntingdon, Pennsylvania (where the author was senior pastor). Hence I can gladly give testimony to the positive impact of Fike's preaching.

At times Earle secures attention by relating personally experienced incidents. However, he avoids the temptation (not always successfully resisted by some preachers) of dwelling excessively on his own pilgrimage. Rather, these personal or familial anecdotes serve to relate the biblical account to the life histories of those being engaged. In natural ways, those addressed are thus helped to see the connection between biblical narratives and their own faith journeys.

The sermonic style is engaging and straightforward, never making a show of the solid intellectual preparation which underlies the messages. Here Fike wrestles with deep issues of the faith, including the problem of evil, the reality of death and the promise of immortality, atonement and sacrifice, and the saving action of Jesus Christ. A parishioner once challenged him with the question,"Why is God so angry that Jesus has to die to make things right between us and God?" Fike's careful answer was the focus of the ensuing sermon.

Any thoughtful believer will find in *A Month of Sundays* resources for honestly addressing and at least partly answering a wide variety of critical faith questions. Sermon titles such as "Grasshoppers and Giants," "God's Tattoo," and "A Warm Finger on a Frosty Pane" promise and also deliver fresh approaches and affirmative responses to basic issues of belief and trust.

Of particular interest are several sermons dealing with the Easter event. How does the pastor make that age-old story come alive again for congregants? In one of the collection's especially creative efforts, "The Year Easter Got Lost," Fike imagines a time when somehow the Easter story was banished from all Bibles around the world. The furor this created and the rejoicing when the story was reinstated led, he relates, to the divine judgment that this was the "Second-best Easter the world has ever had."

This collection can be read, pondered, and studied with profit by Christians of any denominational allegiance. Fike's own sturdy affiliation with the Church of the Brethren (one of the historic peace churches) is revealed most notably by the very last selection, "A Conversation with God," preached just after the outbreak of the Gulf War. The sermon was structured so as to allow the congregation, in essence, to listen in to the deliberation of a pacifist when his nation had just entered international conflict. This gave hearers a meaningful way to focus their own thoughts on the burning controversy of the day.

With great warmth, with lively wit, and with a pastoral heart, Earle W. Fike Jr. has been for many years a faithful and effective servant in congregational and denominational vineyards. By making this collection of sermons available in print, he broadens his ministry to include a much wider number. One can expect that active ministers will be helped by attention to this masterly preaching. Beyond that, all readers concerned with deepening their faith in realistic ways will find here a rich resource.

—Donald F. Durnbaugh
  Professor Emeritus of Church History,
  Bethany Theological Seminary and
  Fellow, Young Center for the Study of Anabaptist and
  Pietist Groups, Elizabethtown College

Author's Preface

Those of us who attend church regularly hear a sermon almost every Sunday. So why publish this collection? The reader deserves a partial answer.

While there is considerable conversation about the effectiveness of the sermon for the community of faith, I remain committed to its centrality in the tasks of ministry. In John 21, Jesus asks Peter three times (with slight variations in wording), "Do you love me?" Each time, Peter says yes. In reply, he is told repeatedly to care for Christ's sheep. If Peter genuinely loves Jesus, he must demonstrate that love by tending the flock, and a fundamental component is committing the time and work necessary to faithfully feed them.

To use a biblical analogy, the house which comprises the total living ministry of a community of faith will have many rooms where the task of ministry is fulfilled. There will be a living room where the life of faith is lived in relationship to one another and the world, a place where individual and corporate sharing is entertained and promoted. There will be a room for relaxation and rest from labors, where sleep renews one for the rigors of daily discipleship. There will be a family room where much of the fun and fellowship of living together occurs. There will be a study where the mind labors intentionally and the imagination runs freely.

Finally, there will be a kitchen, where the community chef goes about the business of feeding Christ's sheep. This book represents a collection of recipes and entrees which were prepared for a community of faith.

The assignment of being a "flock chef" is as profound and contemporary for those of us who are called to ministry in this day as it was for Peter. Providing food to members of our congregations for their spiritual, physical, and emotional health is a demanding task for any of us who respond to the call to minister. My commitment to preaching includes the conviction that if we are required to feed the flock, then we would do well to learn to be the best at the task that we can be.

In bearing the responsibility of "flock chefing," I've been comforted by some words by Robert Farrar Capon in *Parables of Grace*:

> After all the years the church has suffered under forceful preachers and winning orators, under compelling pulpiteers and clerical bigmouths with egos to match, how nice to hear that Jesus expects preachers in their congregations to be nothing more than faithful household cooks. Not gourmet chefs, not banquet managers, not caterers to thousands, just gospel pot-rattlers who can turn out a decent nourishing meal once a week.

Those words are, for me, a kind of contemporary translation of our commission from the Gospel of John.

Despite the daunting descriptions of the scope and limitations of preaching which appear in the Preface Quotes, some of us with the help of God and the inspiration of the Holy Spirit attempt the task of feeding on a regular basis. Those of us who preach every Sunday put our faith on the line weekly. That is both exciting and scary. Our spoken words are heard, absorbed, and taken to heart in whatever way the listener allows.

There are advantages to a sermon that is listened to. It is a one-time event that involves the personality of the preacher and has great potential for dramatic and oral enhancement. The way in which the pastor presents the message is often an important part of our understanding of what is said.

While oral presentations require a particular investment of attention to "stay with" what is being said, they also allow for selective listening. We may tune in and out, depending on how our minds and hearts are engaged. Most pastors realize this is normal, and hope that during the "out" times, the listener is engaged in applying or directing his or her own thoughts to the matter being presented.

A book of sermons puts the pastor's faith on the line in an even more comprehensive way. A book persists longer than an oral event. Words that are heard once may be misconstrued or forgotten, but words that are written exist for the life of the text. So putting a sermon into print can be even more intimidating. There are, however, some advantages to reading sermons. The printed word allows us to ponder, to ruminate, to absorb more deeply.

I am a manuscript preacher who writes sermons in the style I speak. Because my sermons are written out, it has been easy for me over the years to give copies to people who request them. Sometimes people who hear a sermon say they want to have more time to think about what was said. Sometimes they want to share the sermon with a person who might find it helpful.

One difficulty with turning toward more formal publication of material originally prepared for oral presentation has confronted me, however. At the time I preached these sermons it was not as crucial as it is in a published book for me to track precisely where I found material cited or quoted. Now that the sermons have moved toward publication, I have aimed to pin down in as much detail as possible what ideas or quotes I found where, and to give credit where it is due, while needing to be satisfied in some cases with relatively general attributions.

I hope this book will encourage reflection and connect with readers' lives. If these sermons are a way for readers to enter more deeply into the wonder of God's good news, if they are a way for readers to have time to be engaged by and think about their faith in new ways, and/or if they help persons become inspired or renewed in their faith commitment, then this labor will have been worth the effort, and some of my prayers for doing this task will have been answered.

To any colleagues who regularly take on the fearsome but wonderful task of preaching, or to any who are just beginning to study and are in training to grow into this responsibility, let me say that I have found reading sermons prepared by others to be a way of increasing my understanding of my task as a preacher. It is faith-expanding to see how another mind and heart works at communicating the gospel, and it is informative to see the various forms sermons can take.

Many of the sermons I have read served as written tutorials: examples of how to begin, how to progress through ideas, and how to finally arrive at an important place of understanding. Many were good examples of exegetical study and applications. Many provided ideas that would not rest until I had dealt with them in my own way. Also, reading others' sermons whetted my appetite to continue to grow in the quality of my own preaching. If this collection serves that purpose in any small way, then more of my prayers for doing this task will have been answered. And if there is something here that merits the dedication "for the glory of God and my neighbor's good," then the whole of my prayers will have been answered.

I wish to express my profound appreciation to parishioners, to sometime listeners, and to friends and family who across the years encouraged my efforts to communicate God's good news in ways that invited making sense of faith and life and living. I owe a deep debt of gratitude to the good folks at Herald Press, and specifically to Michael A. King, who managed the project on their behalf. Finally, I remain forever grateful to the One who called me into a ministry that included the challenge of regular preaching.

—*Earle W. Fike Jr.*
  Bridgewater, Virginia

A Month of Sundays

1

We Also Run

Ps. 139:1-18; 23-24

Let me introduce you to a biblical track team. These persons hold no world records, and none has ever participated in the Olympic Games. But they really know how to run.

Perhaps the most illustrious member of this team is a man named Jonah. His story is less than three verses old before he is out of the blocks and running—in the wrong direction.

The Word of the Lord comes to the prophet in Jonah 1:1-2. Then the third verse says, "Jonah set out to flee to Tarshish from the presence of the Lord." What follows is an amazing series of events:

- a storm at sea;
- motel arrangements with a sea monster;
- a rather sick experience on the beach;
- the conversion of a whole city of people in record time; and
- a miserable messenger suffering because he was successful, nursing his disappointment in the flimsy shade of a castor oil plant.

"You ought never to run from the Lord!" Can you remember hearing a minister with a brass band voice thundering that at you? I can. I remember fearing what might happen to a person who ran from God, even though sea monsters weren't common where I grew up.

But Jonah isn't alone. There are plenty of other "also rans." Consider these colorful members of the biblical track team:

- Adam, who ran and hid from God in the cool of the evening;
- Moses, who tried to run from his responsibility to lead the children of Israel by overexaggerating his speech problem.
- Jeremiah, who wailed, "Lord, I'm just too young for this kind of job."
- Or Saul of Tarsus, who ran away from what God was saying until he ran into it on the Damascus road.

These also ran. The pages of Scripture are filled with the roster of those who have run the race for God in the wrong direction.

The writer of Psalm 139 must have tried to run at some point, for he says of his experience,

> Where can I go from your spirit?
>   Or where can I flee from your presence?
> If I ascend to heaven, you are there;
>   if I make my bed in Sheol, you are there.
> If I take the wings of the morning
>   and settle at the farthest limits of the sea,
> even there your hand shall lead me,
>   and your right hand shall hold me fast.

There is certainly a different spirit in these verses than we find in jolly Jonah pouting under his plant. Here is the song of one who is happy that the situation is like it is. Here is one who is grateful that there is no way to gallop out of God's range.

Whether we are happy about it, like the psalmist, or displeased by it, like Jonah, the effort to dash away from God must end in failure. But that doesn't stop us from trying.

There are plenty of contemporary recruits for this track team dashing like the devil away from God. Chances are, a look at the roster will reveal our own names among them.

We run in many ways. One is with our minds. Many of us decide around college age that what we've been fed is local church pablum and we're old enough to eat Wheaties. We decide we're too old for religious emotion and sentimentalism, so we become emotional over science and sentimental about ourselves.

Sometimes we run by saying there isn't any God; God is simply a wish created by the human mind. Sometimes we may admit that there may be something in this God bit, but it isn't important enough to get our blood pressure out of whack.. Sometimes our minds run from that which we can't explain, or manipulate, or control. Intellectual running, if it isn't honest, eventually ends in the belly of despair, and life becomes merely a sick existence that finds us regurgitated on the beach of some wasteland.

One of the more common ways of running is to place God in a special compartment of life, penned there in isolation. Every now and then we take out our convictions and polish them up, so the lack of attention to them won't show.

Once when our family was getting ready for company, I was reminded by a person more skilled in etiquette than I am that good silver should be polished before each use. Something that isn't for everyday use, but only for occasional service, must nonetheless be kept looking like it's active all the time.

Sounds familiar doesn't it? One of the ways we run from God is to save our convictions for special occasions and haul them out when we think they will decorate or enhance whatever is going on.

Some of us run from God because running is a habit. When I began working for pay in the orchards of Virginia, my older working colleagues told me that the nickname of our employer was "Speedy." Sometimes nicknames reflect a character exactly opposite of the person. But not in this case. He is one of the few Southern gentlemen I've known who had Yankee genes.

Speedy never did anything slowly. When he walked from the house to the barn, it was a fast walk, between four and five miles an hour. When he loaded hay by hand and you were on the receiving end up on the wagon, it was like trying to keep ahead of a small alfalfa tornado. His cows gave more milk, because they were shamed by how soon he finished putting his hand to them.

Some of us run under the guise of busyness. One way to keep God at arm's length is to be running from this to that at such a pace that there is no time left to recognize God's presence.

The tragedy of this is that many times the things we are busy doing are good things in themselves. But it's terribly easy to be busy with religion and not involved in it. It's easy to run oneself to exhaustion in the church and still be running from what the One who ordained that church is trying to say to us.

Then here is another great way to run—through comparison! "Comparisoners" are expert sprinters. We run from God by saying, "I'm not perfect. Goodness knows, no one is. But then, I'm not the worst either." That kind of talk holds the celestial record for a hundred yard clash with God's intention for any one of us.

We run, even as many before us also ran. But I think an honest survey of where our running gets us must eventually bring us back to the wisdom of Psalm 139.

Essentially the psalmist is saying that it's no use to run, because our stubby little legs can't carry us where God isn't. Whenever our mind even thinks of God, we are stuck with

God. For you see, our very running from God always makes us aware of where God is. Our search for a place without God always keeps us in touch with God's presence.

Now, alongside the fact that we can't get away from God, we need to set one other great gospel truth. No matter how we run, we can't undo what God has done for us in Jesus Christ.

We can turn our back or go in the wrong direction. We can reject the faith, bow at the shrine of New Age theology, or become expert in Zen Buddhism. We can know more about the intricacy of our navel than the doctor who cut our umbilical cord. No matter how we reject God, it is still not enough to undo what God has done in Jesus Christ. No matter how loudly we shout no, God's yes in Jesus Christ is always the final word.

Now, you may be saying, "Good! Thank you, Earle! If I can't get away from God and can't undo what God's done, what is everybody worried about? You've just handed me the best case for eternal security I've been offered for many a day."

While it's true that we can't undo God's work, it is also true that we have to accept it. It works somewhat like a safety deposit box; you need two keys to get to the valuables. Whether your key is used or not doesn't affect whether the treasure is there. But to get to what's inside the box, you have to use your key.

In this case, God placed the treasure and provided the second key. The valuables are always there, but to reach them we must accept the second key and use it.

In his poem "The Hound of Heaven," Francis Thompson wrote these classic lines about trying to run from God:

> I fled Him, down the nights and down the days;
>   I fled Him down the arches of the years;

I fled Him down the labyrinthine ways
    of my own mind; and in the mist of tears

    I hid from Him, and under running laughter.
Up vistaed hopes I sped;
    And shot precipitated,
Adown titanic glooms of chasmed fears,
    From those strong Feet that followed, followed after.

At end of this long poem, there is a moment of revelation as the pursuing presence says to the one fleeing, "Ah, fondest, blindest, weakest, I am He whom thou seekest!"

Having recognized that we cannot run from God or undo what God has done for us, we must also know that for all those who ran before us and for all of us who still run, there comes a time when the futility of running away makes itself heard in a longing for home.

In my first parish experience, I heard a family story that has always touched me. A five-year-old boy had a major misunderstanding with his mother. As thousands of other boys and girls have done in similar circumstances, he shouted, "You'll be sorry; I'm going to run away from home."

His mother, being a wise and insightful person said calmly, "Are you sure?"

"Yes!" he said, "I'm sure."

So she said, "I don't want you to leave. I love you. I'll miss you, but if you're sure, I'll help you get ready."

So she helped him pack a suitcase, kissed him goodbye, and waved to him as he walked up the street. Then she went on about her work, for the street in their little town wasn't the kind of place where you had to worry much about a five-year-old lugging a suitcase that was as big as he was. Nonetheless, she watched out the window as he wearied of his heavy load and sat down on the suitcase.

Chin in hands, he sat there for several minutes. Then she saw him get up and start back. When the doorbell rang, she answered it. As he looked up at her, he bit his lip, then very seriously said, "Hello lady, someone found your little boy."

There comes a time for all of us, when weary of our own brand of running, tired of our negativism, we stand on the threshold of home, lugging life and all its luggage, and say simply to God, "Hello. Here I am. Someone found me."

2

Everybody Makes Missteaks!

Philem. 1-25; Ps. 94:12-19

Before we start, let's settle the business of the title. It's spelled the way it is supposed to be.

Maybe the mistake was mine to choose this bit of whimsy as a sermon title. It is on the subject, as you shall see.

The idea is not original with me. It is one of those bumper sticker pieces of wisdom that I simply couldn't resist. I used to have in my office one of those "plan ahead" signs where the last *d* ran down the side of the paper because there wasn't enough room to finish the word. I like short sayings that have a smile in them, yet contain larger messages than their size might indicate.

Everybody does make mistakes. Some are serious and create real problems; others are mostly embarrassing and are easily remedied.

There are certain audible responses that indicate a mistake. One of my granddaughter Ashley's favorite words was "uh-oh." Anytime she dropped something, spilled something, or created a loud noise, she would say, "Uh-oh."

Most of the time, this is cute when done by a little child. When done by an adult, it can cause considerable anxiety. Can you imagine how you would feel if, while your dentist was working energetically in your mouth, he suddenly said, "Oops!" How would you respond if, in the middle of a two hour session in the second week in April, your tax consultant suddenly said, "Uh-oh!"

Everybody makes mistakes. The Bible's writers know that. The author of Psalm 94 puts it this way: "When I thought, 'My foot is slipping,' your steadfast love, O Lord, held me up." The whole story of salvation in the Bible is necessary because of mistakes.

Interestingly, Paul's letter to Philemon is the shortest book in the New Testament, consisting of only twenty-five verses. In *Charge That to My Account,* H. A. Ironside says that here is the finest specimen of early Christian correspondence we have preserved.

The story can be summarized simply. Onesimus was a slave who belonged to Philemon, a wealthy resident of the city of Colossae. He had run away for reasons that are unclear in the letter, whether because he was rebelling against slavery or because of what he felt was mistreatment. He ran to Rome, which was the place to run if you wanted to get lost in a crowd. There he became acquainted with Paul, became a Christian and became very dear to him—a relationship Paul describes as being like a father and son. In sending Onesimus back to Philemon, Paul said, he was sending his "very heart."

Paul wanted Onesimus to stay with him, because his service was so helpful and faithful. But he sent him back to Philemon and asked him to receive him as a beloved brother. Paul was hopeful that the freed slave would be returned to help him in his imprisonment, but he did not command Philemon to do that. He wanted Philemon's forgiveness to be from his own heart, not out of compulsion.

The story seems straightforward enough, but the subtleties and undercurrents are significant. First, there is Paul's play on words in one of his references to Onesimus. Today we mostly choose names because we like them or they are family names. We don't pay much attention to what the names mean. There are a few exceptions, such as the girl whose mother named her Nevaseena, because her father died before she was born and so he had never seen her. Yet we typically overlook the meanings of more common names, such as Albert, which means "all bright," or Leonard, which means "lion heart."

In Paul's day, names were important. Isaiah meant "the Lord is my helper," and Elizabeth "devoted to God." The name Onesimus meant "useful" or "beneficial." It was not an unusual name for a slave at that time. But Paul played on its meaning by telling Philemon, "Formerly he was useless to you, but now he is indeed useful both to you and to me."

Useful? In what way? To find out we need to understand a little more about the nature of this whole problem.

We are not dealing in this case with a simple little "uh-oh!" Three people are on the spot. Onesimus had in effect "stolen" himself from his master and run away. That was legal grounds for death. If he returned, he risked losing his life or, at best, being severely punished.

Paul was on the spot because he had harbored the criminal and had used his service without Philemon's consent. In this sense, he had become an accessory to the crime.

Philemon was on the spot because he was being asked to test his faith in relation to the cultural laws and values of his day. What would the other wealthy slave owners say if they knew that a thieving, runaway slave was not only pardoned but welcomed as a beloved brother? What kind of precedent would that set?

What about Philemon's pride and wounded feelings? Could he welcome someone who had run away and stolen from him? Now that Onesimus was a Christian, what was expected of Philemon?

Notice how Paul works through all of this. He begins by

recounting the wonders Philemon's faith produced: "The hearts of the saints have been refreshed through you."

Now notice the weight in the next paragraph. Paul says,

Though I am bold enough in Christ to command you to do your duty, yet I would rather appeal to you on the basis of love—and I, Paul, do this as an old man, and now also as a prisoner of Christ Jesus. I am appealing to you for my child, Onesimus, whose father I have become during my imprisonment. . . . I wanted to keep him with me, so that he might be of service to me in your place during my imprisonment for the gospel; but I preferred to do nothing without your consent, in order that your good deed might be voluntary and not something forced.

It gets heavier. "If you consider me your partner," Paul urges, "welcome him as you would welcome me. If he has wronged you in any way," (no doubt Philemon has felt considerably wronged) or "owes you anything, charge that to my account."

Do you understand what Paul is explaining? He's told Philemon, in effect, that "You know that you have become a new person in Christ through my ministry; you would not be who you are if it were not for me; you owe me; I want some benefit from you for Onesimus."

Paul continues, "Refresh my heart in Christ. Confident of your obedience, I am writing to you, knowing that you will do even more than I say."

If ever one friend is working on the emotions of another, we surely have it here. Did Philemon have any real choice? I don't see how if he wanted to remain friends with Paul.

It reminds me of times when my father would say to me: "Earle, you know that we think there are real problems in you going ahead with this plan. We prefer you not do it. But you have the freedom to make your own decision."

This left me with the choice of doing what I wanted to

do or disappointing my parents. An unpleasant choice. But a choice nonetheless.

While making clear what he thought should happen, Paul knew that Philemon still had a choice. Philemon needed to make a legal and social decision in a new and radical Christian context. Paul knew that there was the risk that he would not follow through. Yet the apostle was certain of one thing: if Philemon's new life in Christ is sincere, Onesimus will be safe.

That brings us to one of the major themes in this little New Testament jewel. Paul, Onesimus, and Philemon all knew that when someone becomes a new creature in Christ, that person acts differently. Paul the Christian could not treat Onesimus the way that Saul the persecutor would have. Onesimus the Christian could not act as Onesimus the non-believer would have. And Philemon the Christian would not have been able to treat Onesimus in the same manner as Philemon the heathen master could have.

In Christ, there is a different set of values. When anyone makes a mistake, and all of us do, those values require that the one who makes the mistake face it directly and try to set it straight. Those same values require that the person who is wronged or injured by the mistake respond in a manner that goes beyond the realm of justice into the domain of forgiveness and acceptance.

What we have in this little letter is a magnificent picture of the reality of judgment and grace as essential ingredients in the experience of new life in Christ. And it's all brought down on the simple level of interaction between three Christians who had to address a serious conflict.

It is not easy to do what Paul asked Philemon to do. If you think it's easy, think of the person you most dislike, or the person who most clearly wronged and hurt you. Then think of someone saying to you that you must accept the person as a beloved brother or sister. Maybe you would give up vengeance, maybe you would grudgingly occupy the same community. But treat the person as a beloved family member? That's hard.

Treating a person as a beloved brother or sister does not necessarily mean forgetting, but it does mean open arms, full acceptance. Paul was not talking about love that is an emotion, but love that is a muscle; not romantic love that is a gift, but tough love that does not take us by surprise but is developed through exercise and training. A tough love with no vindictive sharp points and strong round edges of forgiveness. It's not easy.

In my community, we lived through an example of what it means to try and live beyond a mistake. One of our ministers faced a serious personal indiscretion, and the community of faith he served lived through the reality of hearing his confession and accepting him as a beloved brother despite his behavior. There was nothing easy about the necessary judgment of confession, and there was nothing easy about the grace extended to him by his family and his parish.

No one condoned his action. Some found the disillusionment so great that, although they did not personally shun him, their confidence in his leadership cannot be restored. But many who were hurt by it responded in a way that allowed wounds to be healed and relationships rebuilt, so that the work of God in their parish may continue in strength.

Everybody makes mistakes and anyone who is a new person in Christ has to deal with them. The completion of the story of our neighbor church is still ahead. But the story of Onesimus does not end with this little scriptural letter.

We have a good idea as to how Paul's risk turned out. In the second century, Ignatius of Antioch wrote a glowing letter to the church at Ephesus, praising the work of their bishop. And the same play on words used in Paul's letter to

Philemon was used by Ignatius—a pun on the name of the bishop, Onesimus. Since Onesimus was a more common name for a slave than a free man, most scholars believe that the bishop of Ephesus was indeed the same person who was the subject of the letter to Philemon. A risk worth taking, wasn't it?

George Herbert once said that people who cannot forgive in effect burn the bridge that they themselves must cross. Walter J. Burghardt, a Roman Catholic scholar and theologian, compared the unwillingness or inability to forgive to "drinking poison and waiting for the other person to die."

Everybody makes mistakes. And every Christian, as a new creature, has methods and strength for dealing with them. So be willing to forgive by using the muscle of love that is ours through the gift of Christ's love to us.

3

Grace to Grow Up
Eph. 4:1-16

That lovely saint of the Church of the Brethren, Anna Mow, once came to our home. We were discussing her new book, *Say Yes to Life.* "A great many ministers and persons raised in the church are very good midwives," she said. "They know how to confront the individual with the gospel of Christ, and they know how to encourage a new birth in Christ. "But," she went on, "their skills too often end there. For many years, I've been taking up where the midwife leaves off. My task has been to help those who have started on the Christian way to keep on it—and grow in it."

In the familiar Scripture from Ephesians 4, we hear that we have differing gifts which make some of us teachers, some prophets, still others pastors. Yet this text tells us that no matter what our specific gifts are, there is one thing that we are all required to do—grow up!

Our gifts were given "for building up the body of Christ, until all of us come to the unity of the faith and of the knowledge of the Son of God, to maturity. . . . We must no longer be children, tossed to and fro and blown about by every wind of doctrine. . . . But speaking the truth in love, we must grow up in every way into him who is the head, into Christ. . . ."

Sister Anna explained that

Continuous growing seems to be the greatest problem sincere Christians have. The majority of Christians don't

seem to know they can grow spiritually. They seem to
think they either are or aren't Christian. This is as inade-
quate as saying someone is either dead or alive. The person may be just born, or in the strength of maturity, or in
bad shape, and still be alive.

I think she was right. And I suspect that if we probed
deeply into our own lives, we'd have to admit that she had
put her finger on one of the difficulties in our own Christian
experience.

This business of growing in our faith, of being and becoming new creatures in Christ, is hard. It is a rude awaken-
ing when we realize that even though we are Christian in
many ways, we are much the same as we were or have been
for the past five years. The day-by-day battle to actually do
what we deep down believe we ought to do—grow in the
faith—stares us in the face and makes us look away.

Why is it that the gospel is so full of the concept of
growth, and we are so nonplussed by it? Perhaps if we investigate our thoughts on the *how* of becoming Christian, we
may find some of the background for the problem of being
Christian.

The word we most commonly use when we speak of becoming Christian is the word *conversion*. That's what we say
happens when someone passes from life without Christ to
life in Christ.

Conversion means changing from one form to another.
We describe a car with a canvas top as a convertible. That's
because it can change from a car with a roof to a car without
one, or as our daughter used to say when she was small, to a
car without a lid. Conversion assumes that people are convertible—they can change.

One way we change is in our perspectives, the way we
look at life. A young lad and his father whom I both knew
were working on a project in their basement when a power

outage plunged them into total darkness. The young boy began to whimper and then to sob.

Though the father could not see the boy, he spoke to him and moved toward him. In a moment, their hands touched. As the little hand snuggled into that familiar big hand, the little boy said, "Now it isn't dark anymore."

Conversion is a time when we put the hand of our life into the hand of Christ. When we do so, it isn't dark anymore. We are secure. Our perspective has changed.

Conversion also means we change who and what we follow. Before conversion, we may have been looking at a street sign with arrows pointing in many directions. After conversion the many arrows become a one-way sign. Direction is clear if we want to use it.

This means that conversion also changes what we do. A cleaning maid in a motel was asked how she knew she was Christian. She said, "I know I'm Christian because I don't sweep the dirt under the rugs anymore."

All of this together means that conversion changes who we are. I remember reading about a young woman who was dissatisfied and terribly unhappy. Her tone of voice and her actions showed her unhappiness and irritation. She lived under very discordant conditions at home and would have gladly traveled to the end of the earth to get away from her environment.

Sometime later, a friend met her and saw in her smiling face that something had happened. So he said to her, "How are things at home?" "Just the same," she replied, "but I am different."

There is no way to accept Christ that will allow us to remain the same. The world does not change at our conversion; we do.

Aren't these some of the things that come to mind when we think about conversion? I suspect that because we use the word *conversion* and speak of being different—a new creature in Christ—we create a problem for ourselves because all these references seem to limit conversion to a once-and-done experience, to a sudden transformation rather than a process. We think of it as completion rather than as a beginning.

That is a serious mistake. Perhaps we should even cease to speak of conversion and talk about new birth. A child who is born is a new creature, but we expect much less of newborns than of adults. However old we are when we begin life in Christ, we are, for all intents and purposes, spiritual babies. From then on, the challenge is to grow.

Somewhere along the way, we have managed to create a feeling of guilt if conversion doesn't result in a person being mature in Christ right away. That is absurd.

Have you ever watched a little fellow try to match the steps of his dad? He will stretch his little legs way out trying to match the stride of his father, but there is no way he can do it.

Sister Anna noted that many Christians are bewildered. They thought they could walk full stride right away, and are discouraged when they cannot. They stumble over a host of stones because they do not know that these are stepping stones to higher life. They are frightened by the very winds that come to strengthen their roots.

If they think they have arrived when they have just become new members in the family of God, they will surely at best be slow learners. When they are more mature, they may think they are failures every time they find spots on their spiritual clothes. They will not have the joy of knowing that there is a laundry department in the household of God— that there are not only adequate facilities for getting clean, but a holy fabric protector to help prevent stains and to strengthen the believer for the task of growing.

Sister Anna may be suggesting that because we expected too much of ourselves at first, we became discouraged or lazy and began to expect too little of ourselves as the weeks and years went by. We thought conversion was over, and we forgot to say yes to the grace of growing up into mature Christians.

Some years ago, I watched our six-year-old granddaughter, Ashley, learn to ride a bicycle. As young as she was, she understood that she would not be able to ride just because she had been converted into a bicycle owner. She began the learning process with "training wheels" attached to the rear axle. That allowed her the chance to learn several things about how to ride before she had to deal totally with the business of balancing herself.

But she was not satisfied because she knew there was more to bicycle riding than "training wheels." So one day while we were visiting, she said, "Grandpa, I want to try without the little wheels." And so, with parental consent, off they came. Then she had to unlearn something she had learned. She could no longer depend on the little wheels to keep her from falling. Now she not only had to steer and pedal; she had to keep her balance, and she had to learn how to put on the brakes without falling off.

It was a scary process for me to watch. She tried to go too fast, too soon. She forgot to brake when she should have. There were falls, tears, and bandages. But she didn't give up; now I watch her ride confidently and skillfully with the other children on her street.

It's this kind of attitude which we need in our Christian experience: a recognition that the growing process means successes and failures and that we are not likely to become expert overnight. New birth can happen overnight, but maturity is a long way off and something to grow toward and into. And sainthood, that's something few of us ever reach.

Is there a clue in today's portion of Paul's letter to the Ephesians that will help us to understand how we might encourage ourselves to grow into maturity? Paul begs us to lead a life worthy of our calling. He talks about humility, patience, and forbearing one another in love. Then he talks about gifts we have been given as members of the body of Christ. When all the parts are working properly (all members using their gifts and abilities as intended), we will grow into Christ, who is the head. Using the gifts we have is one way to mature.

We know about atrophy—not using a muscle means the muscle will become less useful. To have gifts and abilities and refrain from using them stunts our growth—physically and spiritually.

Sometimes we may read Paul's references to apostles, prophets, evangelists, and teachers and find ourselves thinking, *That list doesn't include me.* So let's take a moment to reflect on gifts all of us have.

Is there anyone who cannot give time for reflection and prayer? Yet how often do we use that muscle? Prayer and meditation are not things we have to be skilled at doing. God accepts them however we offer them. They can benefit the church, our family, and our friends, as well as ourselves.

Is there one of us who cannot smile and be friendly and helpful to others? Courtesy, politeness, and kindness are gifts any of us have. They bless the lives of those with whom we come in contact and help us grow in Christian maturity.

Is there one of us who cannot find a way to be useful to someone else? Each one of us, however limited physically or spiritually, can find someone who can use our assistance. It doesn't have to be a big thing. But it should be something.

There are persons among us who take time to visit and be in touch with those who are shut in. That gift is as important to the body of Christ as some insightful comment in a sermon or Sunday school class.

Is there one of us who cannot learn the art of forgiveness? If we are to treat others as we would like to be treated, is that not a gift we should exercise with regularity?

Finally, there is a muscle of life that doesn't have a Latin name. It's called generosity. And it's a sign of life. To give is to live. Is there one of us who cannot give something of personal resources to honor God? The amount is significant only as it reflects our understanding of that relationship.

You begin to get the picture, don't you? The grace to grow up does not consist primarily in great chunks of meritorious deeds that require special ability. Rather, it consists mostly of faithful attention to little things that any of us can do.

Erma Bombeck, that wonderfully profound and funny writer on all kinds of subjects, once said that "I have learned that silverware tarnishes when it isn't used . . . perfume turns to alcohol and never smells as sweet as when it is used . . . candles melt in the attic in the summer." Then she added, always had a dream that when I am asked to give an accounting of my life to a higher court, it will go like this: "So, empty your pockets. What have you got left of your life? Any dreams that were unfulfilled? Any unused talent that we gave you when you were born that you still have left. Any unsaid compliments or bits of love that you haven't spread around?" And I will be able to answer, "I've nothing to return. I spent everything you gave me. I'm as naked as the day I was born."

Wouldn't it be great if, when we are asked to give an accounting of our lives since the day of our conversion, each of us could say, "I have nothing left over, nothing unused. My pockets are empty. The grace given to me according to the measure of Christ's gift on the day I was reborn has all been used in trying to grow up to maturity in Christ."

Wouldn't that be great? Let it be, dear Lord, let it be!

4

Grasshoppers and Giants
Num. 13:25-14:10; John 21:1-7

The lead article in our local paper for June 3, 1997 began with these words:

> After the explosion, people learned to write left handed, to tie just one shoe. They learned to endure the pieces of metal and glass embedded in their flesh, to smile with faces that made them want to cry, and to cry with glass eyes. They learned, in homes where children had played, to stand the quiet. They learned to sleep with pills, to sleep alone.

These uncomfortable, heartrending words reflected on what happened to some people after the bombing of the Alfred P. Murrah Federal Building in Oklahoma City on April 19, 1995. It was a day when lives were changed, and lives were lost—a day of transition for many.

In a pastoral call, you visit with a young couple who are expecting their first child. The doctor has cautioned them that there may be complications. The fetus is upside down with the umbilical cord dangerously wrapped around the neck. You see fear in their faces.

Days later you visit the healthy parents and child in the hospital. You see on the parents' faces not fear but joy, wonder, relief, and sober realization that they are now honest to goodness parents. You share with them a moment of thanks to God for the arrival of this blessed new life into theirs.

Life is filled with transitions—a series of passages and alterations, some more significant than others. We note the progress, pain, joy, and disappointment of life through the events and happenings that change us.

When transitions come, we can reflect on what has happened to us, but no instant replay allows us to edit what is already history. We can learn from the transition, but we cannot change it. Nor is there anything such as instant "preplay" to help us to know what will happen tomorrow, and thus avoid unpleasant events. We are not as fortunate as the cartoon character Ziggy who stooped down looking through the keyhole in a door. The sign on the door said, "Future."

We know from experience that some events have predictable results. If we are beset by allergies, we know that when the pollen count goes up, we will experience choking sensations, watery eyes, and the explosions of incessant sneezing. We know that if we choose to smoke, our chances of cancer or heart problems increase astronomically. We know that if we are a student in school, and we attend regularly and pass all the courses, we will eventually graduate. But even in all we know, transitions still have unknown qualities that can bring celebration or pain. We are seldom completely prepared for them.

Nothing could have prepared me for a phone call that came to the parsonage at 8:00 one Saturday morning. Slightly miffed that someone would call at that hour, I nevertheless answered in my most kindly pastoral tone, "Good morning, this is Earle Fike speaking."

A lady's voice said, "My husband asked me to call and see if you could realign my front end and balance and rotate my tires this morning."

You can imagine my relief when it became clear that she had the wrong number. I was not prepared for that kind of transition in my job description.

Then there was the case of Homer, a second grader in my wife's class. He wore horn-rimmed glasses, had a Roman numeral III after his name, and was bright and mature for his age. I'm not sure if he carried a briefcase to school or not, but it would have fit him perfectly.

He came into the class one morning and said, in a very low voice, "Good morning, Mrs. Fike."

"Homer," she said. "what happened to your voice? Do you have a cold or something?"

"No, Mrs. Fike," he answered. "I think I'm in the early stages of puberty!"

Now there's a seven-year-old who's ready and eager for a transition.

Life is marked by transitions, changes that both interpret and shape us. In *Passages,* Gail Sheehy says that there are patterns in adult developmental stages, which, when recognized, may be managed as assets rather than liabilities.

One of the important points in her theory is that the potential in any passage cannot be realized unless the passage is named and appropriately responded to. In this context, naming means facing the change, refusing to bury, squelch, suppress, or ignore it.

Once I received a letter from a longtime friend. When I saw the return address, even before I opened the envelope, my mind raced through some of the history I had shared with him. I felt the pain that one friend feels for another.

His pilgrimage had been marked by successes, major contributions, and heavy heartbreak. In the past several years, he had been involved in a complete professional change which required additional schooling and training, and he had to move into a new and highly competitive business world. In this same period of time, he had lived through a marriage separation and a beautiful daughter's emotional crisis that was so severe it required hospitalization.

The letter helped me catch up on family events, but the concluding paragraph brought a tear to my eye: "Personally, I have joined Parents without Partners, I'm taking disco lessons, I'm growing a mustache, and I'm playing tennis. Other than that, I'm the same old guy."

The absurdity of that conclusion said to me, He's facing it. He's naming it. He's responding to it. His passage is painful; it's incomplete, but he's working at it.

While we've talked about the certainty of transitions and the different kinds we may face, we have not yet dealt with the primary questions: How do we face them? With what spirit and with what strength can we respond?

In another time, a whole nation stood on the brink of a transition. The children of Israel had been wandering in the wilderness, moving toward and getting ready for the Promised Land. Now they were on the border, trying to decide whether to go ahead.

Spies slipped into the land, and what a report they brought back: "The land flows with milk and honey, yet the towns are fortified and very large. The people are like giants, and beside them we seemed like grasshoppers."

Then all the people wailed, "Would that we had died in the land of Egypt! Or would that we had died in this wilderness!" In fact, they said to one another, "Let us choose a captain and go back to Egypt."

"Trust God," two of the spies implored the people. "If the Lord is pleased with us, he will bring us into this land and give it to us. . . ."

But "the whole congregation threatened to stone them."

Forget God's care in the Exodus and the wilderness, the people said. We'd rather have our old problems than face what we think the new ones will be.

The story ends sadly. It was forty more years before the transition finally occurred. No one who was twenty-years-old or older at the time of the refusal to enter the Promised Land, ever saw it again.

On many fronts, we face an uncertain future. The national and international giants are real. Television daily puts contemporary giants into our consciousness. Who among us is not threatened by the uncertainty created by:

- political infighting that seems focused on winning rather than serving the people;
- brothers and sisters starving while we worry about diets;
- the use of violence to settle differences or deal with disappointments; and
- physical and moral abuse that touches a large percentage of us.

I was in the office of a man who had worked his way up in management. "Ten years ago," he said,"entering my profession meant you were set for life. Then it changed, and our contracts were renewed on a yearly basis. Now we don't know from one day to the next if we'll have a job."

Is there a more dread-filled word than downsizing? The giants are real!

Our technology and scientific resources are advancing faster than our ethical, moral, and emotional resources can handle. Technology doesn't feel, humans do. How shall we respond to the transition from today to tomorrow? Like grasshoppers before giants? I hope not.

John 21 offers an option. After the agonizing transitions of the crucifixion and resurrection, the disciples were together, trying to decide what to do next.

"I don't know about you guys," Peter said, "but I'm going fishing."

When you don't know how to go on, you go to what you know best. But the apostles' old patterns and old successes seemed not to work. Perhaps the fishing hole had changed; perhaps they were changed.

A voice called from the beach: "Having any luck?"

They answered, "No." The voice said, "Cast the net to the right side of the boat, and you will find some fish." When the net filled with so many fish that they couldn't haul it in, John said, "It is the Lord!"

As they ate in fellowship with the risen Jesus, he told them to feed his sheep. Then they heard words which reminded them of a transition some three years earlier. They heard, "Follow me!"

How might we respond to the giants who frighten us? How might we respond to transitions that change our lives and work? I hope we listen for a voice from the beach that invites us into remembered fellowship and gives us incentive to follow into and through the transitions that come our way.

Do you know the name Lilamani Perera? I didn't either. But some years ago she refused to kowtow to the giant of world hunger. She started a program of saving stamps, the kind we throw away on letters. She sold them through the Salvation Army to dealers who in turn sold them to collectors. In three years, some thirty thousand meals were provided for hungry children in Bangladesh. She didn't slay the giant of world hunger, but she didn't run from it. In her own way, she fed the lambs.

All life is marked by transitions. Some are joyful, others painful or uncertain. But in the spirit of John 21, we have the guarantee of a risen Lord who walks the seashore of our opportunity and offers directions for our transitions.

"Are you having any luck?" he asks. Try another way. Then come, let's be in fellowship. I have two words for you—"Follow me."

Do you hear it? If we hear it, it'is enough. Every one of us who hears and responds in faith can say, "By the grace of God in Jesus Christ, I walk by faith and not by sight through this transition, I don't feel like a grasshopper anymore."

5

A Holy God Who Cares
Exod. 33:12-23

What do we say to ourselves when we are standing on the other side of a major life-changing event—feeling joy in what has transpired, yet still wondering if we made the right decision, still anxious about how it will all work out? God has been with us in this decision, but is God still with us?

What do we say to ourselves when life falls in on us and we aren't sure if the God we thought was with us is really there or not? Wouldn't it be nice to have a little extra divine assurance sometimes?

In Exodus 33, Moses is fresh from the success of leaving Egypt with the Hebrews, yet he is experiencing moments of frustration and doubt about what is ahead. He wants to know more about God, both to feel more secure and to gain additional power for the tasks ahead. Can this be so wrong?

In *The Religious Aspect of Philosophy,* Josiah Royce warns about the inadequacy of an unexamined faith:

> Once in a while, there does come to a man some terrible revelation of himself in a great sorrow. Then in . . . anguish he looks for his religious faith to clothe his nakedness against the tempest, and he finds perhaps some moth-eaten old garment that profits him nothing, so that his soul miserably perishes in the frost of doubt. . . . The only God he has actually had is his own little contemptible, private notion and dim feeling of a god he had

never dared fairly look at. Any respectable wooden idol would have done him better service; for then a man could know where and what his idol is.

Surely there cannot be any great wrong in wanting to know enough about God, that life can be strong, confident, and directed, safe from the frost of doubt.

Samuel Becket, who wrote the provocative play *Waiting for Godot*, has written an even stranger and sadder little play titled *Act Without Words*. A lone actor is seen on a bare stage. This is his world. Offstage, a whistle is heard. Something outside his world has intruded. So he walks to the edge of the stage to investigate. He is suddenly hurled to the floor. Then he very slowly gets up, bewildered, wondering what has happened.

The whistle is heard again, from the other side of the stage. Again he goes to investigate, and again he is hurled to the floor. Then the whistle is heard from above, and he looks up to see fruit descending, but it is just out of his reach. He tries and tries, but cannot get to it. Finally he gives up in frustration.

The whistle is heard again, and a box descends. When he takes the box and stands on it to reach the fruit, the box collapses. At last he sits down. The whistle is heard again, but he no longer pays any attention to it.

That is a sad view of the world, and an even sadder view of the relationship of God to the world. Surely there can be nothing wrong in wanting to know enough about God that we are able to confirm more than some unseen outside force which intrudes in our life, flinging us around without care or compassion.

Yet if there is no problem in wanting to know more, then why was Moses in trouble in Exodus 33? If ever a man was reaching out, only to have his knuckles wrapped, it was Moses. Consider the situation.

First of all, called to do something he didn't really want to do, Moses led the children of Israel out of Egypt toward the Promised Land. They made it to the Red Sea and beyond, a monumental accomplishment in itself. But when Moses went to the mountain for further instructions, the people tired of waiting and made themselves golden idols, a decision that violated the very premise upon which their journey and identity was based.

In a fit of anger, Moses threw down the tablets the Lord prepared for him to share. Then he tried to get the Lord to offer some new understanding of his calling, some confirmation of his commission, some special help for the days ahead. Moses said something like this:

> You've been telling me, Lord, lead these people, but you haven't said whom you'll send with me. You've said, "I know you by name and you have found favor with me." If that's true, then teach me your ways. Remember, this nation is your people.

God answered, "My presence will go with you, and I will give you rest."

> "If your presence does not go with us, don't send us any farther from here. For how shall it be known that I have found favor in your sight, I and your people, unless you go with us? Without your presence, what is there to distinguish the Israelites from every other people on the face of the earth?"

God answered, "I will do the very thing that you have asked; for you have found favor in my sight, and I know you by name."

Then Moses said, "Show me your glory."

The Lord replied:

> "I will make all my goodness pass before you and will proclaim before you the name, 'The Lord,' and I will be

gracious to whom I will be gracious and will show mercy on whom I will show mercy. But, you cannot see my face, for no one shall see me and live. See, there is a place by me where you shall stand on the rock, and while my glory passes by, I will put you in a cleft of the rock, and I will cover you with my hand until I have passed by. Then I will take away my hand, and you shall see my back, but my face shall not be seen."

Do you see the predicament? What a roller coaster ride this conversation must have been for Moses! Yes, I will be with you. Yes, you are special. Yes, you will hear me give myself to you in my name. But no, you will not have power over me. You may not determine what I will do, for I will be gracious to whom I choose, and I will show mercy on whom I choose.

Yes, you may stand here close beside me. Yes, you may see all of my goodness. But no, you may not look me in the face. No, you may not see my glory. No, the best I can do is turn my backside toward you, and let you take a little peep after I have passed by.

My contemporary mind plays tricks with this. I have this image of a kind of divine "mooning," a turning heel and walking away, an act that is more a put-down than a sign of grace. This doesn't fit my understanding of God. There must be more to it.

Have you ever had someone turn their back on you? It rates up there pretty high on the scale of rejection.

One time, I entered my name to be considered for a job that I really felt called to do. The committee said yes, they were thrilled to consider my name; yes, they felt I was an excellent candidate; yes, my previous work was well-done and well-prepared; no, they were turning in another direction. All the yeses seemed of little value when all I could see was the committee's backside as they turned away.

Sometimes, turning your back on a person can get you a severe reprimand. I remember, a time or two in my life, hearing the words, "Young man, don't you dare turn your back on me. You look me in the face."

Yet, surely there can't be anything wrong in wanting to know more about God. What was Moses' problem? Did he have one, or was God the problem?

Some things in the story are clear. It is clear that Moses was asking for special favor. He needed his leadership confirmed again, not only for Israel's sake but for his own confidence. He was asking for special consideration.

And it was clear that he was getting it. The Lord reassured him that he was special, that he could count on the presence of God to be with him. Moses even received the promise of God giving him his name, a very special dispensation. To call each other by name was to recognize a claim which each had on the other; it was in one way a gift of power, but not a gift of control. Moses acquired what he wanted—reassurance, support and loving care.

It is also clear in the story that there is a difference between goodness and glory. Goodness is something Moses could handle. Glory was not. Goodness is the ability to see all of the wonderful works of God and see in them the footprint of God's presence after God has gone by. Glory is the full presence of the unveiled companionship of God. Glory is full knowledge of who God is and what God will do. Glory is knowing it all.

Does this mean that we can understand more about God by looking at what God has already done than by becoming so special that we can fully understand what God is going to do before it happens? Yes, I believe that is partly what it means.

We can learn about God's love and care by seeing the mark of God on creation, by observing God's work in the lives of those around us, and in reflecting on events that have happened to us.

This "afterward perspective" of God is witnessed to by Hagar, who fled into the desert to escape Sarah. The angel of the Lord found her there and told her to return, promising that she would be blessed. Hagar said, "You are the God who sees me, and I have seen the backside of the one who sees me" (Gen. 16:13 NIV).

However, there is a deeper meaning in all of this. In the Bible, *holy* means separate. It means different. It means "other than human."

The mistake Moses made is the mistake Adam and Eve made when they chose to eat of the tree of knowledge. It's a common mistake. We don't like being human and finite. We would like to be infinite, like God.

Moses wanted to see God's glory because he wanted to partake of and be one with God's glory. And the Lord rightly said, "No, you can't do that; we are too different. If I did that, you would die." Moses was a twenty-five watt bulb asking for 250,000 volts of God's glory. If he received what he asked, it would explode him.

So maybe we've looked at this the wrong way. Maybe seeing the backside of God is not an insult but a special privilege granted to the favored. Maybe the backside of God is something seen through the eyes of faith.

If we were like God, faith would be unnecessary. We would know, because we were one with God. So maybe the backside of God is care rather than reproof, love rather than rejection. Maybe turning the backside is not the least God can do, but the most God can do that you and I are able to handle.

Part of the message of this Scripture is that the separation between a holy God and a human person is eternally real. There is no way for us to bridge that gap by standing nose to nose with God. We will have to live a life of faith; we will have to live with mystery. But we do know that God comes our way in loving care. God does all that is possible to help us know and understand without destroying us.

There is no harm in wanting to know more about God. The problem is in wanting to know everything and in feeling irritated, angry, or insulted when that is denied for our own sake.

Next time we want to know more about God than we should, we would do well to remember that we cannot look directly into the sun without damage to our eyes. We should remember the observation by an anonymous author: "God is like the sun, all about us, yet diffused; the one object in the world at which we cannot steadfastly gaze, yet in the light of which we see everything else" (*Pulpit Resource,* vol. 9, no. 2, p. 28).

Whoever we are, we need to know that there is nothing wrong with wanting to know all about God. But beyond that, we need to affirm that we believe in a holy God whose goodness is wonderful to behold, but whose glory, because of loving care, is only available to us from the back. That is because God wants us to know as much as we can and still live in joyful faith—full divine-human relationship.

6

The Big Surprise
Matt. 20:1-16; 25:31-46

On the Christian calendar, the Sunday before the first Sunday in Advent is called the Festival of Christ the King. It is a day to recognize the authority, power, and rule of the one to whom we have given our lives.

This reality is easy for us to forget amid everything that is going on in the world: the continuing threat of terrorism and military intervention, the increase of hardcore racism in our society, financial uncertainty, and the decline of morality in high and low places. Perhaps reflection on Jesus' parable of the laborers in the vineyard and his teaching about the last judgment will give us a helpful perspective about a side of life to which we give little attention.

Some time ago, a state welfare office published a series of quotes from letters of complaint it had received. One woman who meant to threaten the welfare office but used the wrong word said, "If you do not soon send me the money due my husband, I may be forced to live an immortal life." The everyday world situation occupies so much of our attention that we seldom take time to think about the spiritual truth which suggests that we are all going to have to live an immortal life—a life that has reality in a present, coming, and continuing kingdom.

Reader's Digest carried a story about young Matthew, age four, who was eating an apple in the back seat of the car.

"Daddy," he said, "why is my apple turning brown?" His father explained, "Because after you ate the skin off, the meat of the apple came in contact with the air which caused it to oxidize, thus changing its molecular structure and turning it into a different color." There was a long silence. Eventually Matthew asked softly, "Daddy, are you talking to me?" (quoted in *Dynamic Preaching*, vol. v, no. 11, November 1990, p. 21)

The parables are supposed to be simple, easily understood stories. But sometimes when we finish one, we feel like asking, "Are you talking to me?" What seems simple to the teller is not always immediately clear to the reader or listener.

I think that kind of feeling is true of this troublesome story about laborers in the vineyard. Some things about it are familiar. There are employers and employees, wages, hours worked, and clear contracts for working. Such things are a part of our everyday experience.

There is no problem until we get to payday. Then we, like the characters in the story, feel surprised and perhaps even outraged. One person who finished reading the parable for the first time shouted, "That's unfair!"

Let's investigate the story a little. John Dominic Crossan, professor of theology at DePaul, has said that there are a whole series of parables from which we can expect surprises. He calls them parables of reversal because they speak about the advent of a kingdom which will bring direct polar exchanges. That is, it will seem that the good and the bad exchange places.

Here's what he means. In your mind's eye, place a line down the middle of a clean sheet of paper, making two columns, one for the good guys and one for the bad guys in the gospel stories. In the first column put the upright, socially acceptable, economically responsible persons; in the second column, put the untrustworthy, socially embarrassing, poverty stricken, troublemaking people. The columns would look something like this:

Good Guys	Bad Guys
Rich man	Lazarus
Pharisees	Publicans
First seated at table	Last seated
Invited guests	Those uninvited
The dutiful son	The prodigal

In all five of these parables, the good guys on the left were outclassed by the bad guys on the right. In fact, the good were made to look bad, and the bad came out smelling like a rose.

Take one more—the Good Samaritan. In the *good* column put the priest and Levite: staunch, sincere, devout persons. In the other column put the hated Samaritan.

Crossan says there is something more here than a pleasant tale about a traveler who did his good deed. To read it carefully is to know that it is a severe indictment of social, racial, and religious superiority. It is as if the parable is saying, "Take warning." In the kingdom, this kingdom that is and is to be, things may be reversed. What we have thought to be important may not be.

All of this is to say that parables of reversal are a warning that we may be in for some surprises. And the parable of the laborers is just such a story. The surprise is expressed by those who labored all day: "These last worked only one hour, and you have made them equal to us who have borne the burden of the day and the scorching heat."

It seems unfair, even though the story avoids morality. That is, there is no injustice on the part of the master since each got what the contract called for. Nor is there any laziness on the part of the laborers that has to be punished. The big surprise in the story is that everyone is treated equally; and that, for some, equal treatment constitutes unfairness.

Helmut Thielicke, famous German preacher and theologian says in his book, *The Waiting Father*, that

> If those who sweat to earn their salvation are right . . . if fellowship with Jesus were a business transaction with a definite quid pro quo, with accounts of earnings which we present to God and receipts entitling us to entrance into heaven, then it would be shamefully unjust if the person who entered the Lord's service at the evening of life were to receive the same as did all those who toiled and sweated and came home in the evening with bones aching. (117)

Ah, he's on to us, isn't he?

But maybe there is a false assumption here. Maybe the toil of the day wasn't all sweat and backbreaking. Maybe it was joy. Maybe those who were with the master all day (that is, in his service) already had something that those who came last only shared for a short time.

The saints I have known never seem to sweat in their discipleship. I think of Anna Mow, known in some circles for her devotional writings and a life to match. For her, it was as if grace to love and be in relationship with God were joy and fulfillment in itself. She would never have considered working for the Lord a drudgery that must have a carrot of reward hung out before it could be endured.

Or consider this: maybe there is only one reward. It's possible there is only one thing to give in this upside-down kingdom. No place in the Bible says that there is Grace I or Grace II. No place does it say there is acceptable (a), acceptable (b), or acceptable (c).

In the kingdom of Christ, relationships do not come like the mail-order catalogue—good, better, best. When you are in the kingdom in relationship with God and Christ, we have it all. Early or late, we all get the same. Everyone who receives is a winner, and no one is more a winner than another.

Now, if we are persons who relish comparisons, who see our discipleship as sacrifice, as hard labor, and who look with jaundiced eye at others who aren't sacrificing as much (by our own standards), then we may be in for a surprise. The question we ask about why we are all treated equal may be followed by a more embarrassing question at the end of the story, coming back to us from the king of the kingdom: "Are you envious because I am generous?"

Let's move on and look at the story about the last judgment. The king divides all the earth's people, and says to some:

> Come, you that are blessed by my Father, inherit the kingdom prepared for you from the foundation of the world; for I was hungry and you gave me food, I was thirsty and you gave me something to drink, I was a stranger and you welcomed me, I was naked and you gave me clothing, I was sick and you took care of me, I was in prison and you visited me.

To others, he says, because you didn't do these things, "depart from me."

Now we must understand one crucial message in the parable. The countenance of the king is in the face of all the king's subjects. In the plight of our brothers and sisters, in the face of neighbor near or far, we see the face and person of Christ. We ought to be doing these things, not for reward, but because it is the compassionate, joyful, and loving thing to do.

But there is a big surprise. Everyone is surprised, both those who were sent away and those who were offered the kingdom. They all asked the same question, "When was it that we saw you?"

As the question comes from the lips of those who were cast away, the question has indignation, peevishness, and unfairness written all over it, as if they were saying, "Lord, when—*when*? You know that if we had known it was you, we would have done anything. How were we supposed to know?"

As the question comes from the lips of those who were received into the kingdom, there is surprise and disbelief written all over it, as if they were saying, "How can we be rewarded for something we weren't doing for reward?" As if reward comes only for those who search for it, scheme for it, and feel they deserve it because of what they've done.

The surprise in this second story comes with who makes it and who doesn't. When we think about it, the meaning is clear. If we want to be absolutely and completely right, if we must be right and know our righteousness by another's wrongness, if life is a series of decisions as to whether something must be done to get the wanted reward, then we shall be sadly surprised. To ask whether this person or that person deserves our time or our compassion is to already have made the mistake.

Those of us who do what we do as disciples, keeping score to earn the kingdom, will surely find ourselves saying, "When—*when*!" Those of us who go are faithful without a score sheet, because there is enough challenge and joy in the tasks themselves without any thought of building up gold stars, may be among those happily surprised.

Do you remember the elder brother part of the story about the man who had two sons? Imagine yourself amid the celebration over the lost son who had been found. Can you hear the outrage in the question from the elder brother?

Why is it, he demands, that I've worked all these years and you do more for this squandering brother than for me?

Do you remember the answer? "Son, you are always with me, and all that is mine is yours."

The big surprise is that neither the prodigal brother nor the elder brother knew what they had when they had it. Things were different than they seemed.

The biblical scholar Dan Via, in his book, *The Parables,* had his finger on the central point in many of these surprises about the kingdom. The question is "whether we will accept God's gracious dealings"—dealings that "shatter our calculations about how things ought to be" (147).

Maybe hell is receiving the reward and being disappointed in who else receives it. Or worse, maybe it is receiving the reward and being disappointed in what we receive.

Christ rules in a present and coming kingdom that may be different than we expect. It's worth thinking about, trying to understand, getting ready for, even in the presence of crises that seem far more important. Because we shall all be forced to live immortal lives.

7

Not in the Whirlwind

1 Kings 19:1-13; 2 Cor. 6:1-13

Several years ago, three rescuers were trying to help a man who had been injured in an automobile crash. All four people were electrocuted when one of the rescuers backed into a seven thousand volt line lying near where they were trying to remove the driver.

Can you imagine the feelings and questions of the family members? Three people simply trying to aid a fourth injured person, and all four of them die. Why them? Why wasn't the accident at a different place? Why wasn't the power line three feet farther away? What is reasonable, understandable, or just about three people dying because they cared about a fourth? Are there any answers that make sense?

Or listen to the voice of Lamberto Guzman as he reported by ham radio about an earthquake in Peru. The quake lasted three minutes and forty seconds, about the same amount of time it takes us to sing a hymn. Guzman said:

> We were praying and terrified when we heard the infernal rumbling of the mass of mud and rocks falling. All of us who could, ran to higher ground. The injured who remained were swept away. Men and women were holding hands in groups, shouting to God to have compassion. But God didn't hear us.

Are there any good reasons God didn't respond?

Leave Peru and go to Jarrell, Texas. Was God in the tornado that killed thirty-two people? Or what about the arrival of Hurricane Mitch that ravaged the Carribean and Central America? Is God always in any natural or human catastrophes?

We all ask these kinds of questions sooner or later. We all ask them because sooner or later the storm hits us. And it's a good idea that periodically we search the Scriptures and our faith to see what kind of responses we can make.

I believe there may be a clue in the encounter in 1 Kings 19 between Elijah and the Lord. Elijah was fleeing for his life, and he entered a cave on Mount Horeb. There Elijah brooded about what was happening to him. The Lord came to him and asked what he was doing there. Then Elijah's feelings broke loose—all the anger, frustration, sense of injustice and disappointment came flooding out. What we have in verse 10 is a vehement outburst affirming the quality of Elijah's personal zeal for God, his jealousy for God's reputation among the people.

The Hebrew verb *qana* denotes fanatical jealous devotion. The same verb is used to describe God's jealous intolerance of other gods as objects of worship.

It's likely that in addition to being jealous for God, Elijah was worried about his own reputation as a prophet. His success was, in some ways, measured by the faithfulness of the people to God. And they had all forsaken the covenant.

The verb here means to be absent from—to abandon. It is the same verb as the *sabachthani* on the lips of Jesus during the crucifixion: "My God, my God, why have you forsaken me?"

Elijah's predicament was that it appeared everyone else had forsaken God, and he was the only faithful one left. So Elijah was running for his life, and mad at the kind of treatment he was getting for his faithfulness.

Elijah is told to go outside the cave and stand on the mountain, because God will pass by. That is no small invitation. In the Old Testament context, for someone to see God was to risk death. So Elijah knows if he goes out, he may die. If he actually sees God, he will surely not come back.

But listen to what the account says:

> There was a great wind, so strong that it was splitting mountains and breaking rocks in pieces before the Lord, but the the Lord was not in the wind; and after the wind an earthquake, but the Lord was not in the earthquake; and after the earthquake a fire, but the Lord was not in the fire; and and after the fire a sound of sheer silence. When Elijah heard it, he wrapped his face in his mantle and went out and stood at the entrance of the cave.

We know that in one sense, God is in the storm, the earthquake, and the fire. They are a part of creation. They are beyond our control, yet they are in God's control in the sense that they are allowed to happen.

Still, the Scripture is clear in the assertion that God was not in the wind, not in the earthquake, not in the fire, but in a still small voice like the whisper of a gentle breeze. In verse 13 Elijah wrapped his face in his mantle, a sign that he recognized God's presence in the whispering sound. And contrary to all that we might have expected, Elijah was not harmed by this event.

John Gray, a biblical scholar and author of the Old Testament Library Series, once said that

> The unexpectedness of this revelation suggests an important advance in the understanding of God. The revelation of God in an intelligible communication rather than in spectacular phenomena marks an advance in mankind's conception of God as personally accessible and intelligible to humans . . . it anticipates the expression of the divine will in the person of Jesus Christ.

That is to say, God has creative and controlling power over nature, but God has chosen to speak in a personal way rather than in a mind-numbing display of almighty power. In the events of life, whether catastrophe or great blessing, God does not speak to us in the whirlwind of the event itself, but in a whisper, as a still small voice that helps us to begin to interpret, understand, and accept.

In Grand Island, Nebraska, a tornado destroyed over a thousand homes. Pastor Ron Allen of the First Christian Church noted five basic responses (in *Context*, March 1982):

1. Some said, "It was just one of those things." This is a kind of fatalistic view that scarcely deals with the fact of human suffering.

2. Others said, "It was a freak." That suggests that nature is basically friendly, yet we know this is not so. There are weeds that grow, hailstones that fall, and floods that ravage. At best, we might say nature is neutral.

3. A few said, "The devil was responsible and only the faith of Christians in Grand Island kept it from being worse." That answer is unsatisfactory. Good and evil are so intermingled that it is difficult to say, lo, this is the work of the devil, and lo, that over there is the work of God. Who has the authority to make that assessment? Is every one who has a catastrophe a target of the devil?

4. Some parishioners said, "Grand Island is a Sodom, and the storm is God's punishment." Pastor Allen noted that the storm hit the homes of the just and the unjust. But, he noted with wry humor, it would have made a great preaching point if the storm had actually hit only the homes of known sinners and nonmembers.

5. A good many asked "Why did God permit this to happen?" Pastor Allen said he tried the assurances of Romans 8 (all things work together for good for those who love God). But that didn't seem a satisfactory answer.

Over time, Pastor Allen saw two themes emerge in the experience of the people in Grand Island. The first theme was that there is a fundamental brokenness in the nonhuman world. Grand Island was not selected as the victim. Rather, it was a victim by virtue of the natural phenomena in that place at that time. People began to affirm that nature does not select victims but natural disasters occur as a result of random, even accidental combinations of factors.

The second theme had to do with repentance. Natural disasters, while not necessarily created or directed by God, are permitted by God. When they happen, they serve as a reminder that the human race does not live by bread alone. "When a house is picked up and scattered like a seeded dandelion in the summer wind," one person observed, "we are vividly reminded of the fragileness of life."

In addition to those two themes, let me add a third possibility. We know that being alive is a risk in itself. We know that life, as we know it, will end. We know that life is threatened in many ways.

We pray to live long and peacefully. A loved one suffers, and we say the death is a blessing. And well it might be. But is there ever a right time for life to end? We did not choose our birth date, and we do not choose our dying date, unless it be by despair or foolishness.

In the meantime, we know that life includes suffering and loss, pain and threat. We do not like suffering when it happens, but we should not be surprised at it. At the same time, we know that life includes joy, love, and beauty. We should be thankful as we experience the wonders of being alive.

"Several years ago," pastor Margaret Johnston said, "a severe hurricane threatened our home in Massachusetts. Ominous radio warnings that our town lay in its path gave us uneasy hours. As the sky darkened and the wind rose, our young son Blair grew more and more fearful.

"Suddenly, with a loud crash, the power failed. In the dark, I heard Blair's muffled sobs. 'You may just as well calm down,' I said to him. "After all, there is nothing we can do about it.' 'Mother,' he said, 'I know there's nothing we can do about it. But isn't there something we can do about us?'"

Nothing can be done about calamity or disaster. God allows them to happen, but God is not in them. Yet something can be done about us. We can listen for the whisper which helps us to begin to see beyond the storm.

In 2 Corinthians 6, Paul describes God's presence in the midst of hardships that those who follow Christ are asked to endure:

"We are treated as imposters and yet are true; as unknown, and yet are well known; as dying, and see—we are alive; as punished, and yet not killed; as sorrowful, yet always rejoicing; as poor, yet making many rich; as having nothing and yet possessing everything."

When floods hit our valley, I remember hearing that persons said, "We lost everything, but thank God, we have our lives." That's having nothing and possessing everything.

Do you remember a natural catastrophe in the Gospel of Mark, when Christ stood up amid the storm and told it to be still? My New Testament professor, Chalmer Faw, said we make a mistake when we think of Christ as whispering softly to the storm. He more likely shouted at the storm, muzzling it and gagging it with his own God-given strength and power. But he spoke softly to the disciples: "Why are you afraid? I am with you."

Nothing can be done about the whirlwinds, the frightening storms of life. But something can be done about us. We can wait and listen for the whisper, or we can call for the power of Christ to help and reassure us.

Illness can be a whirlwind. I don't speak much about the experience of having two heart attacks and bypass surgery, but as anyone who has been through life-threatening surgery knows, it is a storm. Your life can never be the same.

You can rejoice in returning strength. You can rejoice when you can once again do things you thought you'd never be able to do. You can decide to take care of yourself. You can learn how to say no. You can look at a beautiful sunset, hold a loved one close, and rejoice in the pure thrill of being alive. But none of those things come so long as you stand nose to nose with God, trying to make sense out of what God trying to say in the whirlwind or do in the storm. Thankfulness comes only after you listen for the whisper, only after Christ has stilled the storm.

We need to begin to realize that faith in God does not protect us from catastrophe. Rather, faith helps us to see through and beyond it. We need to realize that faithfulness in Jesus Christ does not protect us from disaster. Yet as the storm is stilled, he helps us to live life joyfully and fully, despite limits or loss.

It is possible to live confidently. Even though we feel that we possess nothing for sure, we can affirm that, by the grace of life given us by God and Jesus Christ, we have everything.

8

Now We're Uneven

Jer. 11:18-20; John 13:12-17; 1 Thess. 5:12-23a

Paul told the early Christians in Thessalonica to "Be at peace among yourselves."

If someone would have said such a thing to Lady Astor and Winston Churchill, it would have done little good. Those two famous people had a continuing battle in later life. Lady Astor once said to Winston, "If you were my husband, I would poison your tea." And Churchill responded quickly, "If I were your husband, I would drink it."

Preparation for communion in the Church of the Brethren used to include a deacon visit in which church members were asked an important question: "Are you in love and fellowship with the Brethren?" The importance of that question had to do with making sure we were in a right relationship with one another before we presented ourselves to God in a service that celebrated our relationship with Jesus Christ. Being "in love and fellowship with one another" certainly has to do with being at peace with one another.

I read once of a five-year-old boy who reacted strongly against his mother's punishment for misbehaving. She had shut him in her clothes closet. When his screaming ceased, she began to hear strange noises, and suddenly everything was very quiet. When she opened the door to see if he was okay, there he sat amid her clothes which had all been torn from the hangers.

"Jimmy," she cried, "what on earth are you doing?"

"Aw, Mom," he said, "this punishment wasn't fair, so I decided to even it out. I pulled all your clothes down and I spit on them. Then I took all your shoes and spit in them. Now I'm sitting here waiting for more spit."

Being at peace with one another is not possible where getting even is the primary motive for action. Have you noticed that whenever someone says to you, "Now we're even," it almost always feels terribly uneven—that you must respond in some way to make the situation more equitable? Payback never seems to be enough when I'm getting even with someone else, and it always seems to be too much when someone is getting even with me.

When we think about it, we know that our anger, hurt, or outrage is not ultimately a true barometer of justice. Our effort to even things out usually precipitates a spiral of increasing hostility.

You've seen it in the schoolyard. Someone playfully hits another person and, surprised at being hit, the second person returns the blow with just a little more force. The first is astounded by the severity of the return and feels obliged to hit back harder. The temperature of the second person rises, and angry words follow, "If that's what you want, take this." Suddenly a brawl progresses.

Getting even seldom works in family, church, school, community, or international relations. The Old Testament, which basically supports a kind of "eye for an eye, tooth for a tooth" justice has flashes of a higher understanding.

An interesting passage is found in Jeremiah 11. The prophet discovered a plot by some of his kinsmen, the priests of Anathoth, to assassinate him by poisoning his food. The reference to wanting to destroy the tree with the fruit recognizes that Jeremiah was unmarried and childless; if his enemies destroyed him, his name (according to the understandings of that time) would be lost forever. It would be as if he never existed.

We can't be sure of the reasons for the plot. Perhaps it was related to the deutronomic reform during the reign of Josiah, early in Jeremiah's career as a prophet. In addition to moral and social reforms, the movement included purifying worship. To monitor and control the quality of worship, all the outlying shrines were to be destroyed and the Jerusalem temple was to be the Holy Place.

With the closing of neighborhood shrines, all the local priests of Anathoth would lose their positions. If Jeremiah supported that move, they might well have wanted to strike him down for contributing to their lost status and unemployment.

In any case, Jeremiah believed that God discovered and revealed the plot to him, so the prophet said, "O Lord of hosts . . . who try the heart and the mind, let me see your retribution upon them."

Jeremiah's plea as to how the Lord will even things out for him goes beyond the individual priests; it included the death of all their sons and daughters by famine so that none would be left. Yet, despite that awful vision, Jeremiah did not take matters into his own hand. He left vengeance to the Lord, because it is God who truly sees into the heart and judges righteously.

Jeremiah used interesting language about being "a gentle lamb led to the slaughter." This is also one of Isaiah's images of the suffering servant.

That, of course, was the connection to the experience in the upper room. There, Jesus did more than model restraint that left the score up to God. He proposed making the score uneven in another way—in an upside-down way. He assumed a posture not designed to make things even through retribution, but through love.

The panorama is before us. From the code of Hannurabi four thousand years ago, which said that "if a son strikes his father, they shall cut off his fingers"; to Jeremiah saying, "let me see your retribution upon them"; to Jesus saying, "You have heard that it was said, 'An eye for an eye and a tooth for a tooth. But I say to you, do not resist an evildoer. But if anyone strikes you on the right cheek, turn the other also; turn the other cheek. . . .'"

In the upper room, Jesus told his disciples to wash one another's feet as he had washed theirs. The teaching and example are outlandish. But there is something there that is ultimately important for being at peace with one another. There is something in turning the cheek, in donning the towel which says, "Now we're uneven," and is content and strong in the saying of it.

Vengeance as a lifestyle is miserable. Yet some people allow themselves to become completely absorbed with evening out the score.

When we lived in Pennsylvania Dutch country, the newspapers carried the story of the saga of a contractor named Lloyd Miller and the widow Salzman. She refused to pay him after he finished her house. She paid what she figured was owed, not what he said was owed. So he wanted the house back.

She refused to either get out or pay in full. They spent eleven years writing checks and sending them by registered mail, only to have them returned. Eleven years of trying to even the score. Eleven years of trying to prove the contract was violated. Eleven years of angry energy and expensive court hearings.

I can't believe it was worth it. I know many TV heroes make us see the value of not being taken advantage of, of making sure no one walks on us, of making sure the score is even. But lives that are full of hate and vengeance seldom leave time for enjoying peace. Harry Emerson Fosdick was right when he said that a life dedicated to paying back—retribution—vengeance—is a life spent as if one burns down his house to kill a mouse. What we lose is far greater than what we gain.

Vengeance isn't always explicitly violent. Few of us get angry enough to spend our life sitting around waiting for more spit. But there is a form of vengeance that I call "bookkeeping relationships." Let me give you an example.

A couple moved into a new community where they made friends with two other couples who were already close friends. They enjoyed being with both couples, and with each couple separately But suddenly they found themselves a third party in a love triangle. They were in the middle of a game they weren't aware they were even playing, and they discovered it in this way. They were returning from a delightful afternoon with one of the couples and were on the way home when the wife of the other couple said: "Don't go by the Henderson's house. If they see us with you we'll have to spend time with them to even it out."

Here was a relationship which was established on a "keeping score" basis. "We came to your house, now it's your turn to come to ours; we called you on Tuesday; it's your turn to call us on Thursday; we sent you an anniversary card, and you forgot ours; what's wrong, have we hurt your feelings in some way?" When they arrived home, the couple held a conference. They needed to find some way to be at peace with one another and the other couples. Neither spouse wanted to come between long time friends; on the other hand, pulling away from both couples seemed not only unfair, but avoiding the issue.

They decided to speak to each of the couples separately. They said something like this: "We're embarrassed and sorry if we've come between you and your other friends; we enjoy your company and want to be with you. But we don't have space on our kitchen bulletin board for a friendship score card on which time and favors and attentions and oversights have to be evened out. We are eager for your friendship, but we will not keep score, either for us or between the two of you. If that creates a problem for you, then we will need to move out of the relationship."

In this case, the situation ended happily. All three couples were able to remain friends.

Bookkeeping relationships are a form of vengeance. They require a "getting and keeping even" mentality. Being at peace with one another means not having to keep score; not having to be even in the give and take of relationships.

Two decades ago, when the Pittsburgh Steelers were riding high in the National Football League, they waved what they called "terrible towels" as a motivational and victory symbol. The towels were waved to show they were better than even with their opponents; they had the upper hand.

But there is something different in the girded towel used by Jesus. There is an uneven quality in the servant role he took.

Richard Foster, the author of *Celebration of Discipline,* sees a difference between choosing to serve and being a servant. Choosing to serve is a now-and-then decision on which there are many contingencies. Sometimes it's what the score is—how much do we have, how much do they have. Do they deserve our help; have they really tried to help themselves; are they worthy of our time or service?

Choosing to serve can be based on how we feel about the person. Have they treated us well? If the score is three snubs to one, then we have two coming.

Being a servant does not allow us that kind of score keeping or selectivity. Servanthood, upper room style, is not an occasional decision. It is a lifestyle.

I suspect that some of our resistance to or hesitancy about taking communion is because we feel we haven't been treated evenly. That is, it's hard for us to receive love when we aren't sure we deserve it. Or, on the other hand, it's hard for us to believe in love if we can't see how we deserve the burdensome troubles that come our way. Or finally, it's hard for us to symbolize love through communion symbols when we feel angry or hurt by something another person has done. Any way we look at it, it seems uneven—unjust.

Isn't it true that deep inside, any confession of need on our own part places us in an uneven position with God? More than that, isn't it true that the gospel itself, in its insistence on salvation by grace and not by works, places us in the uneven position of never being able to deserve what we get? We might be able to be more comfortable in receiving communion if we felt the score was more even—if we felt more worthy, if we felt somehow we tried hard enough that God owed us, or if we felt injustice and wrong acts had been evened out by repentance and forgiveness.

Vengeance and acceptance are God's business. Any score-keeping belongs there. In the meantime, being at peace is being open to relationships with one another.

A servant doesn't keep score; one who chooses not to serve probably will. In becoming servants, we can be at peace with one another because God takes care of all unevenness, and we can relate without measuring sticks. The towel we remember from the upper room is not one we wave in victory or throw in after defeat. It's one we gird on in love and non-selective service.

The good news of the gospel is that we're uneven. It's supposed to be that way, and God in Jesus Christ has taken care of it. But it's our responsibility to live by the servant example Jesus has given. So, brothers and sisters, take a towel. Wave it in the style of the upper room. And be at peace.

9

Irritated Love
Acts 16:16-34

How many different adjectives have you heard used with the word *love*? Blind love, irresponsible love, real love, romantic love, dependent and codependent love, tough love, puppy love. You could probably cite many more examples.

What about "irritated love?" The words don't seem to fit together, yet many experiences might fit.

Take the going-to-bed routine. "Can I stay up a little longer?"

"Okay, fifteen minutes."

"Will you come and tuck me in?"

"Yes, when you're in bed."

"Tell me a story."

"Okay a very short one."

"You turned the light off in the hall when you went downstairs. Will you turn it back on?"

"Okay, if you need it."

There's a pause. "I'm thirsty, can I get a drink?"

"No," the parent shouts. "Now go to sleep!" That's an irritated love response.

Let's begin by making sure we understand what irritation means. According to the dictionary, it is anything that excites annoyance, impatience, or ill temper. It means to anger, aggravate, provoke, or exasperate to a degree less than rage or fury.

To fret is to be persistently irritated. To provoke is to be irritated to anger.

There are two other uses. To irritate is "to make sore or inflamed," like what happens to your eye when a bug flies into it, or what happens to your nose when you continually blow it into a rough handkerchief.

There's one other use of the word: "to irritate is to excite to a characteristic function."

Dr. Francis Glisson, a professor in Cambridge, England, developed what he called the doctrine of irritability of living substances. It's a complex subject, but essentially it means that cell growth is stimulated through irritation. All parts of the body—fluids, bone, fat—are irritable. That is, they respond to irritating stimuli from the brain. Professor Glisson used words like *motivated* and *stimulated,* as well as *irritated,* in developing his theory that energy from the brain moves the body into action and growth.

All of which is to say that irritation in itself is not bad. Irritation can make good things happen. We know in our own lives that some of our most important growth experiences come about as a result of pressure to change, of having to give up something comfortable and take on something new and unfamiliar.

Starting a new job is an opportunity but may also be an irritation. Getting ready to go to college can be an irritation, but the opportunity it provides is worth the aggravation.

Learning itself can be an irritation. Some psychologists suggest that the only way we actually make any progress at all is through crisis. The irritation of some uncomfortable situation forces us to grow. So, we may agree, irritation can be a positive force.

But for now, we want to think of the kind of irritation that gets our goat, that excites us to annoyance, impatience, or ill temper. Loving someone does not preclude irritation.

In fact, the phrase, "familiarity breeds contempt" probably came from the recognition that in the intimacy and proximity of close caring relationships, the possibility of irritation increases. When we can choose who we are with, we can avoid irritating characteristics in others by absenting ourselves from them. But when we live with someone, as we do in families, we are with them in good times and bad times, in sickness and in health, in funny situations and in recurring irritations.

Leaving lights on, leaving the commode seat up or down, refusing to flush, leaving toys all over the garage so that the car cannot go in until it is cleaned up, playing music too loud, tracking mud through the kitchen; slamming the back door, or someone eating all the pie before you get your share—all such things are irritations. You can name your own. Many of them come more frequently in the intimacy and proximity and love of a family situation.

How does irritated love respond? Let's get into Acts 16.

While it's not the main emphasis of the story, there are some clues about irritated love in this narrative. During their stay in Philippi, Paul and Silas and those with them encounter a slave girl who follows them around and who has the spirit of the python. (The pythoness was the priestess at Delphi, who gave oracles from the snake that was sacred to the Greek god Apollo.)

People believed this girl had the gift of predicting the future. In her trances, she could tell fortunes so skillfully that people were willing to pay significant fees to her masters.

Despite her fame, however, Luke does not use the standard verb for prophecy to describe her work. He uses the verb *manteuo*, which elsewhere in the New Testament identifies lying or false prophets.

Some scholars suggest that the girl may have had epilepsy. Others suggest that she only pretended to go into a trance to bilk customers. The text itself does not provide sufficient information for us to know whether her powers were real.

In any event, the slave girl follows Paul through the streets, shrieking at the top of her voice in a way similar to the demons described in the gospels, which were upset at the presence of Jesus. The verbs describing her actions are present participles, indicating she was constantly following them, harassing them, and screaming at them.

At last, Paul's patience is exhausted. Various translations say he was "annoyed" (NKJV, RSV, NEB) or "irritated" (Phillips). Others say he lost his temper (JB), was upset (TEV), or was so troubled he simply couldn't bear it any longer (NIV). So he turned to her and said to the spirit in her, "I order you in the name of Jesus Christ to come out of her." The spirit came out.

Now that she was healed, she could no longer tell the future, so her owners were out of a source of easy money. This made them more than a little irritated themselves. One is reminded of news reports about a woman who sued her doctors, claiming that a CAT scan had damaged her brain and taken away her power to foretell the future.

In this story we have two examples of how to handle irritation. The owners of the slave girl stirred up the people against the missionaries, and had them beaten and thrown in jail. That's a judgment, or justice response to irritation. You gave us a problem; we give you a problem.

Paul's response to the slave girl was a caring and loving response. He was concerned about her condition even though she annoyed and upset him. He healed her and gave her the opportunity to be free from her enslavement, even though she didn't ask him. He did not attack the girl but the evil spirit in her.

We live in a time when we are very conscious of physical and emotional abuse. Hardly a day goes by that we are not confronted by some report of violence or abuse that was apparently set off by some irritation—a domestic argument, a jealous lover, a teenage quarrel, a frantic parent who takes it out on a fussy child. Recently the news carried the story of a woman who tied up and set her husband on fire because he ate her chocolate Easter bunny.

Maybe you have seen the public service commercial in which the stove boils over, the mother burns her hand, the telephone rings, and the baby cries all at the same time. The mother screams into the phone and rushes to the crib. The commercial freezes the picture just as she reaches for the child, and a voice says, "Count to ten before you pick up the baby."

Frustration, anger, and rage may respond one way to irritation. But love should respond in a different way.

We would do well to learn how to respond to irritation without harming the person who is irritating us. When I talk to young couples in premarital counseling, I speak about learning to fight fair. There will be disagreements and irritations in any marriage. It is important that the verbal fight be carried out fairly. One good way to do that is to use *I* statements rather than *you* statements.

Let's imagine a family situation. The wife asks her husband to help her wash windows on Saturday. Although it is not his favorite thing to do, he promises to help.

Friday afternoon, a good friend says, "We're going up to the lake tomorrow morning early to fish. We've hired a good guide who knows where the stripers are; we've got room for one more. Can you go?"

Between window washing and fishing, there is no contest. He says he'll go.

Friday evening, as he goes over his equipment getting everything ready, his wife asks what he's doing. "Elmer asked me to go striper fishing at the lake tomorrow, and since I don't often get that kind of offer, I'm going along." Now his wife is irritated, and justifiably so. How may she respond?

She could respond by saying, "You are undoubtedly the most selfish and uncaring person I know. You are also a liar. You promised you'd help. You are willing to go back on your word to your wife just so you can go fishing. If I fall off the ladder tomorrow and break something, count yourself responsible! What an example you are for our children!"

If she responds this way, how do you think the husband will respond? Likely, from the beginning of the first sentence, he has all but quit listening and is beginning to compose his own defenses: "If you really loved me, you wouldn't get mad over something like this. Windows can be washed anytime, but I don't often get an opportunity to go fishing with a guide at the lake. Besides, you do things because they are important to you, and I don't raise a fuss. How about me having to get the family supper Wednesday evening because you didn't get back from the market in time, and didn't even have the courtesy to call?"

From there on, the argument is all downhill.

But the wife could have said something like this: "I am really angry and disappointed. I accepted your promise to help me tomorrow. I have everything ready. I can't do the windows by myself. It makes me furious!"

Now the husband must respond, not to defend his honor, but to deal with his wife's hurt. He can't call her names, because she hasn't called him anything. She has said how she feels; he must respond to her feelings of hurt and betrayal, not her judgment about his character or who he is as a husband and a father.

Learning how irritated love responds is not easy. But it is possible. I read of a wealthy lawyer who owned eleven antique cars, each worth a lot of money. When he died, he left a curious will. It decreed that his cars should be divided among his three sons: half of the cars to his eldest son; a fourth of the cars to his middle son; and a sixth of the cars to his youngest. A great argument arose among the brothers as to how the will should be honored, and the irritation level was mounting by the minute.

A friend of the family drove up in her new sports car just as the discussion was about to break into a fight. She asked if she could help, and when they explained the problem, she parked her sports car along side the eleven other cars.

"How may cars are here?" she asked.

"Twelve," they said.

So she gave half of the cars, or six of them, to the eldest. She gave the middle son a fourth of the twelve, or three, and she gave the youngest a sixth of the cars, or two.

Then she said, "I believe the terms of the will have been fulfilled. Six plus three plus two are eleven."

But they said, "There's one left over."

"I know," she said, "that's mine."

And she got in and drove away.

There are often ways to deal with irritation without violence if we take the time to work at it. Now days, we have educational courses and seminars and specialists on conflict resolution. Irritated love, New Testament style, worked at that long before it became popular under its new name.

We know that the proximity love places us in, as well as the routine of life, means that in love relationships there will be irritations. Irritations bring responses. But real love, though it may experience irritations, does not destroy or injure because of the irritation. Real love will find a way for confrontation, but it will not physically or verbally abuse another. It will seek out the source of the irritation rather than punish or do damage to the person.

A woman once developed a throat condition. Her doctor prescribed a medication, indicating that during the six weeks she was on the medication, she would need to refrain from using her vocal cords. No talking at all. So for six weeks she blew a whistle when she needed the children, and she wrote notes to give instructions to the family.

At the end of the time, someone ask her about the nuisance of writing the notes. "You'd be surprised," she said, "at how many hastily written notes I crumpled up and threw in the wastebasket before I gave them to anyone to read. Seeing my own words before anyone heard them had an effect I don't ever think I will forget."

Genuine loving responses to irritations can be learned. The gospel encourages us to make use of the unfamiliar meaning of irritation: "to excite to a characteristic function." That is, we should activate the function of love in the relationship that is suffering irritation.

Wouldn't it be nice if we cared enough for those we love to think of ways to respond to the irritation without verbally or physically injuring the person? Wouldn't it be nice if we understood irritation as an opportunity to grow in our exercise of love?

10

Can We Be Born Again?

John 3:1-17; Mark 2:18-22

One of my favorite cartoon characters, Ziggy, is shown tearing the page for the twelfth of the month off his calendar. But instead of the number 13 appearing on the next page, there is a message which says, "A day like any other day." Ziggy's life seems to be one unexplained problem after another.

When I saw Ziggy in this predicament, I thought about Nicodemus. In John 3, Nicodemus comes to Jesus by night for a private tutoring session. Nicodemus is a Pharisee, a learned man who obviously wants to learn more but hopes to do so with as little personal risk to his reputation as possible. He is a dissatisfied man looking for a little springtime for his life.

Jesus says to him, "Very truly, I tell you, no one can see the kingdom of God without being born from above."

Nicodemus responds, "How can anyone be born after having grown old? Can one enter a second time into the mother's womb and be born?"

This is a well-educated man, so we have to assume that his response is not a dumb question. New birth is not a common experience for someone who is old and set in his ways. Every day, Nicodemus tears a page off the calendar of his life and finds a notice that says, "This will be a day like any other day." Strange things like being born again simply don't happen. It is as if he is saying to Jesus: "I hear your words, but they don't compute. Things like that just don't occur."

I feel a little sorry for Nicodemus. He's been the butt of a good many jokes about being stupid, thick headed, or slow. We have this notion that if Jesus had said those words to us, we would have made some kind of positive response: "Great, Lord, that's just what I wanted to hear. I'm ready. Let's do it!" We wouldn't be like Nicodemus, would we?

One Sunday morning, a woman called to ask me about the congregation I was serving as pastor. "Are you born again Christians?" she asked.

To be honest, I hedged a little. Usually that question is loaded and carries certain prescribed meanings for the person who asks it. We did talk about the congregation and what it was like, and I invited her to come visit.

How would you have answered? Do you believe that you can be born again? Do you have any idea what it means to be born again? Do you believe that you, the reader, can become a new person?

I'll let you rest with your own answer. But I suspect it's safe to assume that there aren't a majority of silent yeses among us. We may not ask the same questions Nicodemus did, but there are a lot of things we'd like to know before we turn Jesus loose on us.

Think with me a little about eternal life. Most of us believe eternal life has to do with future life. But within its root meaning in Scripture, eternal life means both now and the future. It's a two-dimensional reality. The Greek word that is translated "eternal" would better be translated "of the age to come."

The ancients divided history into "this present age" and "the age to come." And eternal meant that a quality of the age to come could be experienced and lived in the present age.

Now if that seems difficult to fathom, think of what happens to you when you have something to which you are looking forward. A few years ago, my sister attended a party for around seventy people who were retiring from public school teaching. She was one of the seventy to whom the school district made an offer that was hard to refuse. But despite how committed she was to teaching, it was not a sad night for her. When she talked with me about it, she had only ten days of classroom time left, but she was already living in the joy of what retirement would be like for her. It was clear when she talked about the event, that the future had already become a part of the now.

I once visited with one of my dearest friends, who had been a college roommate. He was in the process of building a new house. He had the blueprints, the contract with the contractor, but ground hadn't yet been broken.

As I sat talking with him, he was already filled with expectation of what it was going to be like for his family to live in their new home. His joy was right now. It may have been in a kind of mental escrow, but it already had such a touch of reality that some of the future was already with him.

The most miserable persons I know are those who have nothing to look forward to. Nothing of the future touches their present with anticipation or eagerness.

Jesus speaks of eternal life as that quality of the future that can be present in the now. In Scripture, eternal life does not have so much to do with length of life as quality of life.

A *Los Angeles Times* article once quoted two Russian scientists as saying that before long, human beings will be able to live for four hundred years (August 13, 1982). We could have a little fun with that prediction couldn't we? Like, how big a cake would it take for four hundred candles? Or what size wallet would it take to carry around the pictures of all the grandchildren, great grandchildren, then great, great grandchildren, and so on.

But beyond our fun, there would be some serious questions? What would the quality of life be if we lived that long? Would the extra years be helpful if we didn't have the faculties to use them creatively? Eternal life, in the scriptural context, has more to do with quality than quantity, although there is all the quantity we can imagine.

So how do we enter into eternal life? How do the old and new get together? A parable from Mark 2 gives a picture. Jesus says:

> No one sews a piece of unshrunk cloth on an old cloak; otherwise, the patch pulls away from it, the new from the old, and a worse tear is made. And no one puts new wine into old wineskins; otherwise, the wine will burst the skins, and the wine is lost and so are the skins; but one puts new wine into fresh wineskins.

Don't get hung up on the wine. This is not a text on total abstinence or social drinking. Nor is it a biblical commercial for preshrunk fabrics or multiple-stitch sewing machines. The saying raises the question of a relationship between the old and the new.

In gospel times, new wineskins had an elastic quality. They stretched and expanded with the fermentation of the wine. An old skin had done all of its flexing. It had already expanded to its limit. If new wine were put into an old skin, the wine would ferment and explode the container that had lost all its stretch.

There is a simple truth here. The new can't be contained in the old. That seems obvious to us—or is it? It means the new life can't fit in the old framework. It says the potential of new devotion can't exist under the rigidity of old habits.

How hard we work to put a little nip of something new into the wineskins of old ways. We'd like to season life with some new sprinkling of faith to give zest to our ordinary fare. We know deep in our bones that we need to do something that will tell us we are trying, that will tell us there is something alive and exciting left for our life. Yet we don't want anything that will really shake our equilibrium.

I saw an intriguing cartoon which consisted of a picture of a skunk. The caption under it said simply, "I treat all my friends the same."

That's an admirable quality isn't it? But with a skunk we wish it weren't so. It's true that a skunk is a skunk. You can call him by his Latin name, but he's still what he is. You could feed him a salad of wilted chlorophyll bathed in expensive perfume, and he'd still be recognizable as a skunk.

Most of us are that tenacious with the character of our lives. We'd like to be able to bathe in the faith and still be like we used to be. Jesus says we can't do it. Put the new wine of the gospel in an old wineskin, and we are likely to lose the wine along with the skin.

Not everything one learns in college is absorbed from classroom lectures. During our first fall in school, my roommate and I decided that being a students ought not to deprive us of good old fashioned Virginia apple cider. I'm not talking about this thin pale stuff that sits on grocery store shelves. I'm talking about the real McCoy, no preservatives added, with all the "leavins" left in—the thick kind that when you shake it up you can't see through it.

We bought three gallons from a local cider maker. We put one out on the window ledge so the fall weather would keep it cool. It didn't last long, so then we put the second one out there too. The third gallon was stashed in our clothes closet, which incidentally shared a common wall with the radiator for our room. The second gallon lasted longer became we became slightly more temperate in the amount consumed each day.

But it was the gallon in the closet that surprised us. The lid was unsealed and the radiator provided extra heat. You can imagine what happened. There was a tremendous explosion, and our entire wardrobe (not very large, but important to us) was decorated in lovely brown cider splotches.

The parable in Mark 2 teaches the same lesson. If you put the new wine of eternal life into an old inflexible container, you end up with a mess.

The quality of life we are talking about requires elbow room. Some of our greatest frustration may be trying to put something new into something old. Like Nicodemus, we'd like to feel different and yet be the same.

Julia Esquivel wrote a book of poetry titled *Threatened by Resurrection.* The concept implied by her title is an intriguing one. We're afraid when we realize that something has to die for newness to occur.

Up to now, we've neglected one part of the parable. We haven't considered that part of the passage that has to do with the mending chore—the part of being born again that is able to use some of the old.

Jesus says that an unshrunk patch is not for an old garment. My wife Jean tells me that it might not tear the old garment, but if it didn't, it would certainly buckle it, cause it to gather, and in short be unsatisfactory.

There are two ways to look at this. If you want to preserve the old, if it's worth saving, then you want to do quality patching. You shouldn't sew something to the good life that isn't tried and tested. If your faith has meaning, use the same kind of patch as the original material. It would be easy to wrinkle or destroy a valuable garment if you sewed on a flimsy patch. I've seen spiritually restless people do that.

On the other hand, some clothes aren't worth mending. Have you played the "wear hole, tear hole" game? I played it first at the age of eleven while working on a farm.

Sometime during the morning, I snagged my jeans and put a hole about the size of a quarter just above the knee. As we were riding along back to the field after lunch, one of the adult workers sitting beside me saw the hole, pointed to it, and asked, "Wear hole or tear hole?" Not knowing how the game worked, I gave an honest answer: "Tear hole." Which is what he did. He put his finger in the hole and tore my pants leg from above the knee down to the bottom.

When I protested, he said, "When I ask, 'Wear it or tear it?' you said, 'Tear it.' So I did." What was left of my pants wasn't worth patching. The pair had to be replaced with something new.

The patch and the wineskins speak the same message. Something old is not the best companion for something new. The wine of a new birth calls for a new container. It's a truth whether we apply it to ourselves personally or to the body of Christ in which we worship and live. We should preserve only that which has proven itself to be in so central to the life and teachings of Jesus that we cannot afford to give it up. Anything else—procedure, style of worship, tradition—should be open to change.

When actor Don Murray first broke into movies, he used to spend time with the Brethren because of his experience as a Brethren Volunteer Service worker in Sardinia. I once heard him talk about a movie he wanted to make.

It was the true story of a prizefighter, who made his way up through the syndicate, throwing some fights, winning some. He made the usual rounds of the high life—nightclubs, bars, call girls. He almost destroyed himself. But one day, this fighter (whom he called Tommy) had a new birth, a genuine Christian conversion. Something so real came into his life that he became a changed man.

Don said he already had the closing scene worked out in his mind. Tommy's old girlfriend sees him on the street, and calls out, "Tommy, Tommy!" But he keeps on walking. She runs to catch up with him, takes hold of his arm, turns him around, throws her arms around him, and says, "Tommy, it's me." He looks at her, gently takes her arms and holding her at arm's length, he says, "I know. But it isn't me."

Do you believe in the springtime of the soul; in the possibility of new birth? I do. In fact, I believe being born anew happens many times in the life of a Christian.

I could have answered yes to the woman who wanted to know if I was a born-again Christian, but my guess is that we would have missed each other. Being born again is all about growing in the faith. Every time we fail, miss the mark, ask forgiveness, and begin again, we begin as a newborn. Every time we are moved to make a new commitment to Christ to try harder, we are born anew.

I don't think people or congregations have to get up every morning and tear the page off the calendar and see the words, "A day like any other." It is possible to be eager for, rather than threatened by, the possibility of being born again. It is possible to be touched by the quality of the "age which is to come" in this present day.

But we can't do that and be the same. We have to change enough to be able to look in the mirror and say to ourselves, "I know you, but it isn't me anymore."

11

God's Tattoo
Isa. 49:8-18; Matt. 6: 24-34

Most of us know what a tattoo is. It's art work done on the skin.

A tattoo is made by pricking small holes in the skin and inserting pigmented color into the wounds. When it heals, the color stays permanently. Earliest indications of tattooing go back to Egyptian mummies from around 1300 B.C.

Whether we personally think they are attractive or not, tattoos have an important characteristic—they are permanent. You can't forget where you've left a tattoo. It goes with you. A tattoo can't be changed depending on the day or season. You can't say, "I'll wear it this winter, but not next summer on the beach." Wherever you are, the tattoo is also there. It literally becomes a part of you—an identifying feature.

Because tattoos are permanent, one does not flippantly make a decision to "get a tattoo." Occasionally you hear of someone getting one on a dare, but usually there is some good reason for having and displaying a tattoo.

According to Scripture, God has a tattoo. The specific text is Isaiah 49:16: "I have inscribed you on the palms of my hands."

The setting is this. Israel is in exile and in deep despair. The life of the Israelites has collapsed, and they have almost no hope for the future. They believe God has forsaken them and perhaps even forgotten about them. They are lower than the tummy of a three-foot dachshund.

So along comes the word of the Lord to the suffering:

> They shall not hunger or thirst,
>> neither scorching wind nor sun shall strike them down,
> for he who has pity on them will lead them,
>> and by springs of water will guide them. . . .
> Sing for joy, O heavens, and exult, O earth;
>> break forth, O mountains, into singing!
> For the Lord has comforted his people,
>> and will have compassion on his afflicted.

Have you ever noticed how hard it is sometimes to sing hymns of praise when you feel broken and depressed? Persons who feel beaten down and hopeless often react in one of two ways when they hear good news. Some people get angry. Others simply fall into a deeper depression.

Can you hear Israel's response to this promise of love and care? I can imagine some of the people saying: "What is this? The Lord has forsaken me. Cut out this talk about help, comfort and compassion."

Perhaps others responded like this: "Go away. Leave me alone. The Lord has forsaken me. Don't add insult to injury."

But the word comes back in response:

> Can a woman forget her nursing child,
>> or show no compassion for the child of her womb?
> Even these may forget,
>> but I will not forget you.
> See, I have inscribed you on the palms of my hands;
>> your walls are continually before me.

Now what jumps out of this Scripture at me is the quality and persistence of God's relationship to Israel. Let's look first at the quality. Somewhere I saw this passage of Scripture referred to as "outrageously anthropomorphic." This phrase means outrageously ascribing human qualities to the nature of God. Of course, one of the most effective ways we learn something is to experience it in our own terms. God knew this in the incarnation. So we will let the images stand as they are, outrageous or not.

This is one of the biblical passages that ascribes beautiful feminine images to God. Would a mother forsake a nursing child? We certainly hope not. Yet we know that once in a while a mother does forsake her children; we know that once in a while there is a mother who abuses her child. So the Word says, "Even if mothers may forget who they are and how they should act, I will not forget you. To prove it to you, here, look, I have you tattooed on the palm of my hand."

That's a strange place to have a tattoo, isn't it? But let's think about it for a moment. If creation came from the work of God's hand, then the tattoo, the remembering of all humanity, was a part of creation itself.

Or think about it in this way. Any time God stretches out a hand toward us, it will be there for us to see. The tattoo is there for God to see if the hands are turned up in the sign "come to me," or "here, I have something for you." And the tattoo is there for us to see if the outstretched hand seems to be saying: "Wait; hold off for a moment; this is not something you want to do."

The tattoo is there for us to see in the outstretched hand that gives a blessing. That is, when times are hard and the hand of God seems to be against us, the tattoo is visible to us if we will look for it. When times are good and more to our liking, then the tattoo is next to all that the hand of God gives and receives.

Perhaps you remember the popular song of the 1940s, "I've Got You under My Skin." That's what God says. "I've got you inscribed in the palm of my hand." It's like saying,

"The memory of you, concern for your welfare, is a part of all that my hands do. You are a part of me."

As we said, tattoos are permanent, and they are usually worn for a good reason. God's tattoo is to let us know that God remembers; God does not forget us. The memory of us is a part of all that God does. That's the quality of God's relationship with us.

Now quickly to the persistence. You'll notice the style of this Scripture is somewhat like a disagreement. God speaks; humans speak back, then God speaks again. There is communication going on over a difference of opinion. We often speak about the importance of communication: in the church, in our families, and especially in interpersonal relationships such as deep friendships or marriage.

But I believe we need to make an important distinction between communication and communion. The Otis Elevator Company developed an elevator called the Elevonic 401. When you walk in the door, it says, "Good morning!" (Or "Good afternoon," whichever is correct.) Push the button to go up to the sixth floor and it says, "Floor six, coming up!" When you exit, if one of the doors happens to close a little too fast and nudge against you, it says, "Excuse me."

The Elevonic elevator has the capacity to speak 111 words. We can rightly say it is communicating with us, but there is no communion going on. There is no interchange.

The result of communication that is two-way, listened to and understood by both participants, is communion. That is, when communication is communion, we enter the world of the other person.

One winter, my wife Jean and I attended a couples workshop on communication in marriage. One of the skills we had to practice was a procedure called a "shared meaning." A shared meaning is a commitment to a procedure that has a strict set of rules. The one who has something which needs to be shared has the responsibility to do it as clearly and as succinctly as possible. The one listening has the responsibility to repeat back, at frequent intervals, exactly what he or she has heard and understood the other to say. If the feedback is not the same as the communicator intended, the first person tries again and only goes on to another point when he or she feels understood.

This can be a cumbersome process if used legalistically, but it is extremely helpful. I think it's helpful because it recognizes several important things. It recognizes that communion between persons takes intentional time. It recognizes that communion between persons requires listening rather that thinking what you are going to say in response while the other is talking. It recognizes that really understanding the other is important in any relationship. It recognizes that communication, which is communion, takes persistence and hard work.

One year the congregation I was serving held a special seminar on ministry with the aging. The part of that experience most people felt was particularly helpful and exciting was what was called a "life sharing" segment. This was simply a time when older persons were given twenty minutes to talk about their life, their family, their experiences—to share anything they wanted to about themselves and what was important to them.

At first, some of the older persons were timid. They weren't sure it was right to take that much time focused on themselves. But after the exercise was over, those who had shared said it was unusual and meaningful to talk and have someone really listen to what they were saying.

The style of this Scripture about the tattoo shows not only a quality of remembering, but a commitment to the kind of persistence necessary for communication to become communion. God does not turn away and quit on dialogue. The tattoo says we will not only be remembered and not forgotten; we will also be heard and understood.

One day the cartoon character Ziggy is out in a life raft, alone in the middle of the ocean. Looking up at the heavens, he shouts, "What did I ever do to deserve this?" A great voice shouts right back, "Do you want a list?"

These verses in Isaiah promise us better treatment than that! When we feel down and are ready to shout that God has forgotten us, a great voice responds: I have not forgotten you. See, you are tattooed on my hands. Let's talk until we understand each other.

12

The Highest Common Denominator

Ps. 21:1-6; 1 Cor. 1:10-17

Mrs. Monterey's fourth grade students were deep into working with fractions. They weren't doing well. Many were hiding behind their books, hoping not to be called on.

"Robert," she said, "Take 13 1/4 from 29 1/3 and what's the difference?"

"Yeah," he said, "that's what I say. What's the difference? Who cares anyway?"

In case you've forgotten, here's a quick refresher course on fractions. If you want to take 13 1/4 from 29 1/3, you have to understand that the numerals under the fraction line are denominators. To subtract one fraction from the other, you need to find the lowest common denominator. If you convert 1/4 to 3/12 and 1/3 to 4/12, you can subtract.

The principal of the lowest common denominator is sometimes used in fields other than mathematics. In this age of political correctness, the phrase or word which is all inclusive, which covers everyone, and offends no one, has become not only an art but sometimes a requirement.

Take the matter of public prayer. Duke University chaplain William Willimon says that

> I went through a stage of attempting to pray generic
> prayers. Rather than address the God of Abraham, Sarah,

Isaac, Jacob, and Jesus, I called on 'that divine force which touches our lives.' After one of those prayers, a student at Duke University told me I sounded more like a crew member of the starship *Enterprise* than a Christian minister. (Quoted in *Context*, June 1, 1992)

In an article in *World Magazine* addressing "Pluralism and Politeness," R. Albert Mohler Jr. spoke out against requiring those who pray in public to find the lowest common denominator language. Mohler, a Baptist minister, was invited to pray at a local school board meeting. He was asked at the same time if he knew how to pray in public. When he inquired what that meant, he was informed that the school board did not want to exclude or offend anyone of another faith who might be there.

Translate that to mean that the minister was not supposed to use the name of Jesus Christ or any other openly Christian allusion in the prayer. Then what did the Board of Education want? That in public prayer, a Christian minister should sound like a Jewish rabbi, or like a New Age guru, or maybe like Mr. Rogers at bedtime.

The National Council of Christians and Jews, an organization I learned to appreciate when we lived in Chicago, jumped on this nonsensical bandwagon. They issued a pamphlet titled, "Guidelines for Civil Occasions: Public Prayer in the Pluralistic Society," which says: "Prayer on behalf of the general community should be general prayer. General prayer is inclusive, non-sectarian, and carefully planned to avoid embarrassments and misunderstandings."

Mohler says in response:

There is no lowest common denominator between the religious faiths present in America. The guidelines proposed by the NCCJ are as out of date as they are arrogant. (If they chose to do so) Muslims could be offended by any reference to God as Father; Buddhists by any mention of God as creator, and atheists to any reference to God at all, even "the Ground of our Being."

Genuine pluralism means the openness of the public square to all truth claims and faiths, each put forth with integrity and conviction. Real tolerance means honoring the other's right to speak from his or her conviction. This new cult of sensitivity hankering for the lowest common denominator means never having to say you are sorry because you would not possibly say anything worthy of offense.

I remember a story about the way one Christian leader handled the assignment to pray at commencement exercises at a public university. The leader ended his prayer in Jesus' name on the ground that Christians are now, along with so many other religions in our pluralistic culture, members of a minority group rather than an imperialistic majority. When an enlightened faculty member criticized the naming of Jesus, the Christian leader responded that Christians are entitled to their distinctive beliefs and rituals along with adherents of other faith traditions.

Do you begin to get the point? The search for a common denominator may be necessary in mathematics, but there is something tragic and wrong about the search for a common denominator into which all our faith precepts must be divided. Such an effort reduces us all to religious nonentities.

What does this have to do with Paul and the Corinthians? Bear with me a little. There is a subtle way in which the lowest common denominator mentality works in the church itself. There are scads of persons in the church who believe that the Body of Christ must be uniform; that if it is true to its Lord, it will be in one hundred percent agreement. No waves; not even a ripple; no one offended; no one angry.

For such persons, the scourge of the Christian faith is represented by differences of opinion. They see any disagreement as a fracturing of the body, a weakness devoutly to be avoided. The older ecumenical movement emphasis on "that they all may be one" failed to catch our enthusiasm because we assumed it meant some kind of lowest common denominator organization in which we would all be required to assent to some kind of same insipid belief and practice.

Notice how close the word *denomination* is to *denominator*. The word denomination is defined as a name for a group or class of things which have common characteristics.

Have you ever ask why are there so many orders within the Roman Catholic Church and so many denominations within the Protestant church? One reason is because we inherently resist any requirement which threatens to put us into any lowest common denominator of faith and practice.

Differences of opinion within an organization threaten us. If we can find people who agree with us, we feel at home. If people don't agree with us, then we start a new church, a new denomination, a group who will represent our truth. We seek out and convert others to our perspective.

But even within a bona fide denomination, a fraternity where there is basic agreement, we are threatened by differences of opinion. Like some of our Jewish brothers and sisters who believe that if on a single day, all of the Jews live in compliance with the Torah, on that day the Messiah will come. So too there are Christians who seem to believe that the day we have no difference in the way we believe or the way we practice our faith, only on that day can we truly call ourselves the body of Christ. Depending on who is doing the feeling, only on that day can we feel that we are truly Brethren, or Methodist, or Lutheran, or Mennonite.

You begin to see where we're going, don't you? Paul is upset at the Corinthians, for he has heard there are factions, cliques of squabbling people. The NIV says "divisions"; the RSV "dissensions"; the NRSV "quarrels." The Greek word implies a tear in the fabric and thus an injury to the whole.

These early church cliques have been formed, not around theological issues, but around leaders. Church history teaches us that most splits in the church came not from basic theological issues but from persons who were seeking a power base from which to wield their influence.

In Corinth, there were four such parties. The fact that there was a Paul party, implies there was opposition to the apostle. Apollos seems to have impressed people with his preaching brilliance. Cephas was probably never in Corinth, but perhaps some were there who knew him personally or felt his name created an authority which would give their position power. Charles Wolfe has suggested that the members of the Christ party probably considered themselves to be the only genuine Christians—the spiritually elite.

Some believe the language used here indicates that the divisions may have been along lines of the wealthy and powerful versus the poor and the powerless (*Homiletics,* vol. 5, no. 1, p. 15). The reference to Chloe's people reporting the situation may refer to a group of slaves who are apparently on "Paul's side." The other names are obviously rich men—Crispus, Gaius, and Stephanas—wealthy householders.

The poor, such as Chloe's people, were most likely associated with some wealthy householder. Thus, slaves, servants, freedmen, and other struggling workers who were dependent upon a few wealthy households might become a built-in circle of political supporters for those who were rich. Not unlike the family struggles which are present in some local churches in our own day.

In any case, it is clear that the discussions were not dialogue about deep spiritual issues. Rather, they were arguments about who was right and who was wrong, who was in and who was out, who really had the power.

Paul's spiritual blood pressure is high! Is Christ divided? Such quarreling is tearing Christ apart. Or maybe Paul is asking, "Is Christ divided out among you—parceled out in pieces?" A Christ in pieces is certainly not the Christ Paul represented in his preaching.

In an article on "Sectarian Division and the Wisdom of the Cross," Ronald P. Byars suggested that Paul's point was that, "Communion in Jesus Christ is of such high priority that loyalty to parties and persons must take a decidedly lesser place" (*Quarterly Review* 9, Winter 1989, pp. 65-96).

Paul is clear. We must not, by such actions, empty or void the cross of Christ of its power. We are to be joined together, united.

The Greek verb (*katartizo*) was used in medicine for setting broken bones and in the fishing industry for repairing nets. I believe that when Paul spoke of being united in the same mind, he was talking about living in the harmony of the central commitment to Christ rather than complete uniformity in practice or complete unanimity in belief. It is possible to disagree and bear witness to one another for the upbuilding of the body without generating hostility. Such harmony fosters movement toward the truth.

But when we draw lines of privilege or place between ourselves, when we struggle for power or influence over one another, when we create dissension through innuendo, gossip, or destructive confrontation, we are indeed diminishing the power of Christ. When we shut others out, we at the same time shut ourselves in. Paul points out that when we break the bonds between one another, an unexpected consequence is that we break the bonds between ourselves and Christ. That is, in Christ, we can have differences of opinion, differences in belief, but we cannot focus on Christ and at the same time seek to destroy our brother or sister in the faith.

It is as if Paul were saying, do not succumb to the temptation to search for the lowest common denominator into which all our differences can be divided. Give your allegiance and devotion to the highest common denominator into which we can all be undivided.

Thomas Troeger, one of the better contemporary teachers of homiletics, has a parable about dissension in the local church (see *The Parable of the Ten Preachers*). The Reverend Jason Kirk, pastor of Clyde's Corner Church is in trouble. Long before he came as pastor, Cedric Clyde, a very successful farmer and the patriarch and founder of Clyde's Corner Church, out of thanksgiving for God's goodness, donated for the raised chancel behind the pulpit a "red horsehair couch whose rich color and ornate design he thought would brighten the front of the church."

Time passed and that couch became the subject of a bitter debate between members of Clyde's family who wanted to keep the couch where it was and newer members of the church who thought that "old Victorian Leviathan" had no place up front in their plain but handsome sanctuary. Pastor Kirk said: "Every sentence I put in the air, I see them weighing whether it is ammunition for their side or the other side. Here I am preaching about the love of God, and everything I say is filtered through a single question: Is the pastor in favor of the red horsehair couch, or is he against it."

The solution was not a letter from the apostle Paul to the Clyde Cornerians. Nor was the dispute settled by a sermon by the pastor, nor by a church retreat focusing on conflict resolution.

Pastor Kirk, perhaps by inspiration from the Holy Spirit, got agreement in the congregation that they needed to refurbish the church parlor. He pointed out that Cedric's couch was coming unglued and the veneers were splitting because of the extreme temperature changes in the sanctuary. His idea was to have the couch repaired, then placed in the parlor, which was kept at room temperature all week because it was used almost every day for group or committee meetings.

The church at Clyde's Corner came together. All of Cedric's relatives agreed to the plan. The new young members donated money for the entire project, including money for new chancel furnishings and the cost of framing a portrait of Cedric Clyde to hang over his couch.

When the redecorating was completed, the congregation gathered one Sunday for the dedication. Reverend Kirk led in prayer and Florence Clyde, the oldest living member of the family, unveiled the plaque. Then the congregation proceeded to the sanctuary and dedicated the new chancel furnishings.

I think the apostle Paul would have applauded the church at Clyde's Corner. The congregation found a way for people's concerns to be dealt with without destroying the people. Their unity in Christ helped them to find a way to agree despite disagreement.

No one had to lose by changing into the lowest common denominator into which they could all be divided. All they had to do was recognize the highest common denominator in which they were all undivided, and other matters fell into place. It's a good thing to remember—in the church at Corinth, in Clyde's Corner, or in whatever congregation in which you happen to live and serve.

13

The Grace of Wrath
Ps. 90:1-12; Eph. 4:25-5:2

Imagine that you hurry into a supermarket on a Friday afternoon. Grocery shopping is not one of your favorite things to do in the best of circumstances, and today you are trying to push through a narrow aisle with a cart that has a wobbly wheel and insists on pulling to the right.

You run into the heels of an innocent shopper who is stooped over trying to discover the unit price of tuna. A hasty word of apology is spoken, but the look says more than the word. When you finally get to the express line, someone cuts in front of you with more than ten items. The person argues about two coupons that are past their expiration. Then you discover that this customer has chosen several unmarked items, which means that the checkout person has to send a runner to get the correct price.

When finally you dash out of the door into the wind and rain, your grocery bag splits wide open. Anger may not even be an adequate word to describe your feelings—maybe rage (story adapted from Glendon Harris in *Pulpit Resource*, vol. 13, no. 3, p. 21).

We not only live with personal irritations but with societal anger. A newspaper in Wichita, Kansas, carried a report describing how people blockaded a clinic, a child hit a policeman in the mouth, and numerous persons went to jail to express their anger over abortion.

Domestic violence and child abuse are on the increase. Nationally, mothers have maintained a strong voice to influence laws to prohibit driving under the influence of alcohol through an organization they chose to name MADD.

I listened to a discussion recently between two persons and decided that it must be open season on elected officials. I myself have vented my wrath about the unnecessary and cruel postponement of delegated tax funds because of procrastinating politicians.

In the sixth century, Pope Gregory divided all the sins he could catalogue into seven categories. One of these was anger.

Anger is an experience known to us all. Not only do most of us try at any cost to avoid someone else's anger, we do not like to talk about wrath, either as a reality of life with which we must deal or as a biblical truth portrayed in the very nature of God.

Every now and then, we meet a person who seems to be energized by being abrasive and angry most of the time. Such persons go through life with their thermostat set on hot.

People like this are relatively rare and are objects of distant and careful scrutiny. They are not persons we like to be close to and are certainly not examples we desire to emulate. Wrath embarrasses or scares us. It's something we'd like to get over, not get into.

Yet the Bible talks about wrath, particularly God's wrath. What comes to mind when you hear someone use the phrase "hellfire and brimstone?" I'd guess you think of a particular kind of sermon you remember hearing in church or on television.

Jonathan Edwards preached the most famous such sermon on July 8, 1741 in Enfield, Connecticut. It was titled "Sinners in the Hands of an Angry God." Here's an excerpt:

This that you have heard is the case of everyone of you that are out of Christ. That world of misery, that lake of burning brimstone, is extended abroad under you. There is the dreadful pit of the glowing flames of the wrath of God; there is hell's wide gaping mouth open; and you have nothing to stand upon, nor anything to take hold of. . . . The God that holds you over the pit of hell much as one holds a spider or some loathsome insect over the fire, abhors you, and is dreadfully provoked. . . . O sinner! Consider the fearful danger you are in. . . . It is a great furnace of wrath, a wide and bottomless pit, you are held over in the hands of that God whose wrath is provoked and incensed as much against you as against many of the damned already in hell . . . you hang by a slender thread. . . .

That's one view of the wrath of God. Some writings and works of art from the Middle Ages are equally gruesome.

There is, of course, an opposite view. Aristeas, writing in the Apocrypha says, "God rules the whole world in the spirit of kindness and without wrath at all." Marcion, an early Christian heretic, was ousted because he felt the view of the loving, gracious God found in the New Testament was antithetical to the view of God in the Old Testament. Because of this, he refused to treat the Old Testament as canonical.

The most common Hebrew word for wrath, human or divine, is *aph*. The literal meaning of the root is "nostril" or "nose." Among the ancient Hebrews, the nose was seen as the seat of anger. The phrase "slow to anger" literally meant "long of nose." That should be some comfort to some of us!

Remnants of this image persist into our time. Flared nostrils are still a sign of anger, and when someone starts to exhibit wrath, we say, "Don't get your nose out of joint."

In the Old Testament, there is a real difference between human and divine anger. Human anger may be just or unjust. Divine anger is always justified.

Most of God's anger results from human thwarting of God's will. The Chronicler summarizes Israel's whole career up to the exile as a history of scorn for God's Word.

But it's interesting to note that in the Old Testament, where the term for wrath is used in connection with God, the name of God is always *Yahweh,* the covenant God. Wrath is always related to love and caring.

"You only have I known of all the families of the earth," Amos 3:2 says; "therefore I will punish you for all of your iniquities."

From an Old Testament perspective, when God's gracious love is ignored, then that love most show its wrath. Even so, the loving faithfulness of God often constrains the anger, as in Hos. 11:8: "How can I give you up, Ephraim! How can I hand you over, O Israel?"

In the New Testament, there is only one place where the gospels explicitly attribute anger to Jesus. Mark 3:5 says, "He looked around at them with anger; he was grieved at their hardness of heart. . . ." The writer of John makes clear that the coming of Jesus was an act of love and that the Son came not to condemn the world, "but in order that the world might be saved through him."

The major thrust of the gospels is good news. Still, Jesus treats divine wrath with full seriousness, not as if he relishes it, not to frighten or scare, but to encourage decisions and actions that will help people to respond to, rather than miss, the full love and grace of God. Instead of dangling us on a thin thread over the fires of hell, Jesus gives us the image of the waiting father who welcomes the son back from the hell of separation. The focus of the good news is not angry judgment, but long-suffering and everlasting love that never quits waiting for acceptance.

We see then, that God's wrath is the reverse side of God's love. We know how close the two emotions are. Somerset

Maugham said that the line between love and hate is as fine as a razor's edge. Hate is wrath that has no love left in it.

Television replays old *Cosby* shows. In one of them, little Rudy used her dad's new juicing machine despite strict warnings not to touch it. She put grapes in it without a lid, and the kitchen was soon a mess of speckled purple skin and pulp. When she was found out, she said to her dad, "Are you mad at me?"

"Yes, very, very, mad," he responded. "But come here." And he took her in his arms. While he was holding her close and she was beginning to smile at how easy this was going to be, he said firmly, "But you still have to clean up the mess."

Biblical wrath is understood as discipline or necessary judgment. It is never equated with hate, because wrath without any love is an impossibility for God. Wrath may be painful, but it is never evil. Wrath is grace, because it is always in the context of divine love—a sign of God's care.

For us humans, anger is a normal emotion. Unfortunately, most of us know only two ways of dealing with anger—to express it destructively or to suppress it.

Some psychologists, convinced of the hazard of suppressing anger, used to suggest that wrath was healthy. Anger generates adrenaline, we were told; it energizes; it makes a person feel alive. So express wrath, "let it all hang out." If another person got hurt in the process, that was their problem. The important thing was to preserve our own health by venting our anger.

However, psychologist Carol Tavris has said that expressing anger doesn't let off steam, it actually makes you angrier. Couples who try to fight their way to love exacerbate the tension. Nor is all the fuming good for circulation. In fact, angry people are more likely to self destruct physically and mentally (in the form of depression) than well-tempered persons (Maddocks).

In his book *Anger and Assertiveness in Pastoral Care*, David Augsburger suggests that emotions are neither good nor bad; they simply are what they are. Moral judgment begins not with the feelings themselves, but with the behaviors and actions that ensue.

Augsburger indicates that the right to be angry responsibly is essential to people's experience of their own worth and human dignity. Persons have worth because they are worthy, and no behavior increases or decreases the person's value. Whether we are angry or calm, succeeding or failing, hating or loving, apathetic or excited, we are persons of worth. So unless we value anger, we devalue the person. We must learn how to receive it from another and how to manage it within ourselves.

More than this, any relationship that involves trust must allow for anger. Trust is seldom experienced as genuine where anger is regarded as a threat, or where the expression of anger is prohibited lest it lead to a rupture of relationships. One of the most trustful things we can do is grant loved ones the right to be angry without making them feel that the anger threatens the relationship.

Augsburger provides a suggested pattern for dealing with anger. Recognize it—that is, respect the freedom of persons to exhibit anger. Validate it—that is, respect the dignity of experiencing the emotion and physiological reality of anger. Clarify it—understand and respect the explicit causes or demands of the anger. Simplify it—seek natural, neutral, narrow, and mutual definitions of the demand. Finally, negotiate. That is, cancel inappropriate demands, hold to appropriate demands, and negotiate some mutual solution.

Augsburger gives an example. Steve Carney was a high school teacher who was asked to give up his present chemistry classes and to teach biology courses for which he had no graduate preparation.

Carney dropped into Pastor Nielsen's study during lunch break. He was furious.

"I'll be seeing the principal in an hour, and I plan to give him a piece of my mind," he said. "It's criminal to move me into another field with only two days to consider the offer before contract renewal. They're playing dirty, and they're going to hear it."

As he spoke, the pastor noticed how disconnected his arguments were, how he rambled from central concern to peripheral gripe without the slightest awareness of how confused his thinking appeared to be.

"Before you confront the principal," the pastor suggested, "use me for a rehearsal. Make your speech to me."

Carney made a trial run.

"Now narrow the issues. Focus on what it is you really want."

He tried again.

"Now, state your demand in as neutral terms as possible," the pastor says. "Suggest its benefits for both you and the school."

By the time Carney left, he had channeled his anger into a manageable presentation. He was able to state the issue as an understandable difference of opinion between persons. He was able to describe it in language that is neutral. He could address the problem from his perspective in a focused way and can propose a negotiated solution.

I believe such managing of wrath fits Paul's simple instructions. "Be angry," he said, "but do not sin; do not let the sun go down on your anger."

Translating that into contemporary language, we might say Paul was encouraging us to admit that anger is a part of life—something we all experience. Be angry, he said, because he knew we cannot refuse to be angry. And he knew sometimes it would help us to deal with injustice and wrong.

Be angry, he said, because he knew that anger is usually a sign of caring. We don't get upset about things that don't really matter to us.

Be angry, he said, but don't sin. That is, don't be mastered by your wrath; master it.

And "Don't let the sun go down on your anger," Paul said. Which is a practical suggestion that anger should be dealt with up front and as directly as possible.

Sometimes postponing wrath is a way of dealing wisely with a situation. We may need time to think more clearly. But sometimes, to sleep on anger is to avoid it. Tomorrow it may not seem important, so we think we should just forget it—only we don't. The residue of feeling will stick to our psyche like flies to fly paper. And the next time a similar experience occurs, the emotional freight is multiplied.

Sometimes we sleep on anger to prolong it, because we cherish it or want to nurse it. We want it to last. Isn't it amazing the power we give other people over our lives if we insist on remaining angry at them? Isn't it amazing how much time we spend on wrath, how much of what we decide to do is controlled by remembering and nursing anger? Alexander Pope once said, "To be angry is to revenge the fault of others upon ourselves."

In the New Revised Standard Version, the biblical reference Ephesians 4:25-5:2 appears under the heading "Rules for the New Life." Paul knew that anger is a part of being human. Though anger is not easy to deal with, he believed—indeed expected—that Christians living in the new life in Christ would be able to be angry without sinning.

Hate is anger without love. Anger without sinning is anger in love; it's recognizing, validating, clarifying, simplifying, and negotiating the anger.

If we are able to manage our wrath in love, then we join God in the ability to make a grace of wrath.

14

They Knew It Was the Lord
Jer. 32:36-41; John 21:1-7

We have a knotty little problem to struggle with here: post-resurrection appearances. Some people are outraged at any conversation about them; some are puzzled about them; some are too sophisticated to give them any credence. Others have questions they would never think of asking publicly.

For those who sharply distinghish *then* and *now,* it's not as much of a problem. But for those of us who believe that the New Testament witness to a resurrected Lord means that Christ is alive and may yet meet us, the questions of how, when, and how we will know it seem to stay with us.

Suppose you come home from work and greet your spouse with a usual expression of affection. "How was your day?" you ask.

"Good—really special," your spouse responds. "I met the resurrected Lord today!"

Wouldn't you turn your head and wonder what he or she meant? Wouldn't you want an explanation? Wouldn't you be a little concerned about the mental health of your spouse?

Post-resurrection manifestations are not usual occurrences. Still, if we have a mature resurrection theology, we should be able to speak more openly, more assuredly, less apologetically about experiencing the risen Lord.

Let's start with this breakfast on the beach in John 21. The chapter begins, "After these things, Jesus showed himself again to the disciples. . . ."

The basic meaning of the Greek *ephanerosen* is the emergence of something from darkness or obscurity until it can be seen. It is usually used in the passive voice, but here the voice is active, meaning that Jesus chose to reveal himself.

A good analogy would be our contemporary experience with instant cameras. We take a picture, the camera spits out a piece of paper, and after a few minutes an image begins to appear. At first it is fuzzy and unclear, but as we wait several minutes, the photograph becomes well defined. The picture has emerged from something obscure to something visible. It has revealed itself. That is the kind of process of revealing that the Greek text would seem to imply.

But there was apparently a problem, even back then. Verse four says plainly that "just about daybreak, Jesus stood on the beach, but the disciples did not know that it was Jesus." He revealed himself, yet they did not know him.

The failure of the disciples cannot be explained by physical distance; they are close enough to be able to hold a conversation with him. It cannot be too dark, for the same language in Matthew 20:1 means the beginning of the day when it is light enough to work. The problem seems to be that the resurrected Lord has a changed form. He is different.

This was not the first time the resurrected one remained unrecognized. When Jesus first appeared after the resurrection, Mary Magdalene mistook him for the gardener. When she recognized him after he spoke her name, she said to him, "Rabboni." She seemed to hope that the relationship would resume as it was before, but Jesus forbade her to touch him. He was in a different form.

Mary recognized him when he spoke to her. The disciples on the road to Emmaus recognized Jesus when he broke bread with them. The disciples on the beach recognized him when he helped them with their fishing task and ate with them. One could well preach a sermon on recognition and revelation in the eucharist and in the catching of fish, that is, in the Love Feast and in the missionary activity of the church.

In addition to Mary Magdalene, the disciples on the road, and those aimlessly fishing at dawn, we should note one other person who saw the resurrected Lord—Saul of Tarsus on the road to Damascus. Paul's loss of vision, is a metaphor for lack of comprehension. He was able to begin his life of missionary activity only when he was able to comprehend the living Lord.

Athough Jesus revealed himself after the resurrection, people who should have known him immediately did not. Perhaps they were not looking for him, were not expecting him. Or perhaps he was in such a changed form that they could not comprehend immediately that it was Jesus.

Now let's ask a different question. Is it possible to see something that has no touchable form? Is it possible to recognize something that may not be immediately recognizable by another person? I think it is.

I personally like puzzles—all kinds of them. Sometimes I have success with them, sometimes not. But I do not know exactly how to tell you what happens when I suddenly "see" the solution.

Another person might be watching me work on the puzzle, and when I say, "I see it," they may say, "Well, I don't." They might say, "What took you so long?" In case they don't see it, perhaps showing the solution will help the other person comprehend it. But meanwhile, did I see it or not? I think I saw it, even if the other person couldn't see it.

If you are a student you may have similar experiences with math or chemistry problems. You work at comprehension, yet cannot understand something. Then suddenly you

see it. It is clear. And you can't understand why you didn't
see it earlier.

Or maybe you have a knotty problem in your business.
You worry and fret, and you can't see your way out. Suddenly
you get an idea and you see how to work through it. You
comprehend. You recognize the solution.

We see a person, and we say, "There is a really happy person." But what could we take along to prove to someone
else that the person we saw was happy? We can hardly preserve a smile by putting it in the freezer to be hauled out to
make us happy on a grumpy day. Happy, sparkling eyes are
not a touchable form. We see them, but we cannot preserve
them. Only the image of them is in our mind.

We see a person we do not know and say, "There is a person." We see someone we have known and loved and we say,
"There is a lovely person." What is the touchable form which
allows us to see the distinction between the two persons?

The point I'm trying to make is that in our day, it is possible to see something which has no specific touchable form.

So, if the form of Jesus is different, how shall we recognize him? If he is trying to reveal himself even in our time,
in continued post-resurrection appearances, what shall we
look for to help our comprehension? What shall we look for
to move us from "they did not know that it was Jesus" to "it
is the Lord"?

I once heard homiletics teacher Thomas Troeger tell a
story at a seminar on preaching. During the time he was in
seminary, he met and fell in love with a wonderful young
woman. But there came a day when circumstances made it
necessary for her to leave. He went with her to the bus station, and it was a tearful and sad parting. Depressed and-
lonely, he stopped at the lunch counter for a cup of coffee.

He was sitting there, lost in his own thoughts, when into
the coffee shop came a bag lady. Bent over, dressed in rags,

she climbed up on the stool just around the corner from him. She ordered a cup of coffee, and there was one "day-old," flaky doughnut left under the plastic dome. She lifted the lid and laid the doughnut by her cup.

Dr. Troeger said he hardly noticed her as, overcome with sadness and grief, he just stared into his cup. Suddenly, she reached over and patted his cheek.

"Things will get better, son," she said. "Meantime, you look like you could use half of a doughnut. I'll share mine with you."

She smiled as she broke it and offered it to him. Dr. Troeger said, "I recognized Jesus in the breaking of that doughnut."

We often repeat the little truism "seeing is believing." Maybe some post-resurrection experiences are the opposite. Maybe "believing is seeing." Believing in Christ, Thomas Troeger saw him in the kind and friendly breaking of bread in the bus station coffee shop. He knew it was the Lord.

In the Academy Award winning movie *Gandhi,* there was a scene I found particularly gripping. A Hindu man went to Gandhi, who was lying on his bed, weak from fasting. The man was in emotional shambles.

"Help me!" the man cried out. "I have killed a young Mohammedan boy because the Muslims killed my son. But I cannot sleep; I cannot forget. I do not know how to live with myself."

Gandhi said quietly to him, "I know how you can have peace and forgiveness. Take a homeless young boy about so high, and raise him as your own son. Only be sure it is a Mohammedan boy, and you must raise him as a Muslim."

The man looked at Gandhi, then buried his head in the bedclothes and wept. Believing is seeing. When I saw that, I recognized something of Christ in Gandhi's style and the prescription he gave.

When Jesus said, "Just as you have done it to one of the least of these who are members of my family, you did it to me," it can mean nothing different than that in the face of our neighbor, we behold the person of Christ. That should not surprise us, since love of neighbor is the second commandment, equal in importance to love of God.

Love of enemy is a form of love of neighbor. It isn't easy. Any neighbor, friend, or enemy is a potential form for meeting the risen Lord. Exciting! Frightening!

I heard historian Clarence Kulp once comment about the architecture of the old Brethren meetinghouses. His comment reminded me of one of the seven houses that were a part of the Greenmount congregation, where my Grandmother Myers attended. There was an elder's table at one end, but the congregation was divided, men on one side and women on the other, and they sat on sloped risers facing each other. Kulp's thesis is that for traditional Brethren, Christ was not found in the altar or the worship center, but in the sister and the brother—in the community of faith. In facing one another, we also faced our Lord.

One of the ways we are able to see Christ in our day is in the brothers and sisters around us. Any kindness, any thoughtfulness, any expression of love is a revelation, a beholding of the risen Lord. Any need, pain, or loneliness, any hunger or cry for help, is a moment for recognizing Jesus—a time to say "it is the Lord!" Let no one, not one, say there are no post-resurrection appearances anymore.

15

Togetherness Without Conformity

Num. 11:24-29; Eph. 4:1-16

Not long ago, my wife Jean was looking through an old box of pictures and found among them a note written by our youngest son when he was about seven years old. It was a little home made card, with tiny paper flowers glued here and there. The printing was irregular, as first efforts often are. It said, "Roses are red, violets are blue; to the best mom in the world, I love you."

Discovering that little note was like finding a treasure that we had somehow mislaid. To find it was to relive an experience and know it again.

We're living in a time of great concern about what the church believes and how it lives out those beliefs. Regardless of the particular denomination, within the church there are hot-button issues that, when pushed, immediately drive us to positions that are as far apart as we can get, positions that threaten our feelings of togetherness and community.

Is there a way for us to be together in commitment to Christ without conformity in practice? Is there a way for us to be at peace with one another amid diversity? If there is a way, is it a strong style of living in Christ or a copout? We need to think through these questions because we will surely have to confront some of these issues we have not yet faced.

I tried to think back to earlier controversial issues in the Church of the Brethren and how we survived them. The Annual Conference paper on biblical authority came to mind as something of a model that we have mislaid. Remembering it was not as touching and dramatic as finding a handwritten love letter to Mom, but it is, in its own way, a treasure we ought not to forget. Since 1979, that paper has allowed Brethren to live in fellowship with one another while at the same time strongly disagreeing about methods and understandings of biblical interpretation.

The paper is not only important in what it says but in its style and spirit. It includes eight affirmations about the Bible; all begin with "We affirm. . . ." After each affirmation there is a paragraph that begins, "but we are not agreed on. . . ."

Toward the end of the paper, there is a section called "holding one another in love and fellowship," which is as much to the point of being Brethren as any nine paragraphs of print I know. It's all about togetherness without conformity, how to be at peace with one another amid diversity.

Before we look further at this important document, go with me on a little journey into a somewhat obscure story in the book of Numbers. The story, in chapter 11, is about Moses, Eldad, and Medad.

Moses was discovering that leading the children of Israel was no small task. The administrative burden was getting to be more than he could handle. So he asked for help. God told him to select seventy elders for special commissioning.

The seventy went outside the camp, perhaps to the location of the tabernacle, and there God descended in a cloud to install them in office. Some of the very essence of God's spirit, formerly given only to Moses as a mark of his office, was bestowed on each of them. The spirit moved them to prophesy in ecstacy; probably glossolalia. The Scripture says they did it once and no more, probably signifying that one time was all that was necessary to prove to the people that the seventy had the authority to exercise their calling as Moses' helpers.

But then the plot thickened. Two men, Eldad and Medad, of whom nothing else is known, had the same experience even though they remained in camp and were not present for the service of commission. They were among the elders listed, but they were not among the seventy chosen. So here, two outsiders received the gift of the spirit, and they weren't even at the service.

Now Joshua was not Moses' personal aide for nothing. Although he was not one of the elders, he was Moses' right hand man and he was already sharp in terms of community politics. He saw that the gift of the spirit to the seventy elders did not diminish Moses' authority. They received the gift through the mediation of Moses and, therefore, were clearly subordinate to his leadership. But if two received the spirit directly from God, then they could be understood to have the same relationship with God as Moses. And this might tend to diminish the authority of Moses, to say nothing of the power of his first lieutenant!

So young Joshua got a little riled and advised Moses to forbid them from prophesying. Moses rebuked him for his display of personal ambition: "Are you jealous for my sake? Would that all the Lord's people were prophets, and that the Lord would put his spirit on them!"

Would that all the Lord's people were prophets! That strikes a familiar chord in Brethren heritage. From our beginning there has been no creed, no rigid solidifying of the Spirit's leading, but rather the conviction that through study of the Scriptures and openness to the spirit, all followers might be prophets. Any disciple may receive new light. In Brethren tradition, that light is always tested in the context of the community of faith.

The job of faithfulness is a heavy load in our day, even as Moses' administrative job was. The spirit can be shared with many, so that the work of the one we follow can be done in a variety of ways. We all have a prophetic function, or as the reformers defined it, we are a priesthood of all believers.

That's the foundation from which our church and our Annual Conference operate. It provides the basis for the historic 1979 paper on biblical authority.

"How can we hold one another in love and fellowship," the paper asked, "when there exists a diversity of attitudes among us about the way in which Scripture was given and its interpretation?" The paper continued:

> The way is found in the nature of God's creation, through the example and teachings of Jesus, through the examples of our early Brethren, through acknowledging our human limitations in understanding, and through being open to the leading of the Spirit who draws all members of Christ's church together. Despite essential unity, diversity is God's pattern in creation. God's delight in variety is expressed in countless ways.(Psalm 104) To those who walk in the Spirit, varieties of gifts are given. (1 Cor. 12:4) Conformity is humanity's pattern. It is the way of the world to try to force individuals into a uniform mold.

The paper noted that Jesus denounced the religious establishment of his day, particularly the Pharisees, for doing this. The document observed that there have been times when the Brethren have fallen into the error of insistence on rigid conformity, when church members were forced to agree or risk being disfellowshipped until they confessed the error of their ways.

"It is a mark of the Holy Spirit," the paper continued, "that we can hold one another in love and fellowship even though there is diversity among us. . . . Christian love requires—

- that we acknowledge the integrity and worth of those brothers and sisters with whom we cannot totally agree;
- that we make every effort to understand one another by keeping lines of communication open, by listening to, hearing, and responding to our brothers and sisters;
- that we be willing to test our perceptions and understandings with the gathered church;
- that we be open to the counsel of our brothers and sisters;
- that we behave in a way that builds up the church;
- that we be obedient to Jesus Christ;
- that we not attempt to gloss over our differences but we face them honestly and work at resolving them "with patience, forbearing one another in love, eager to maintain the unity of the Spirit in the bond of peace;" and
- that we hold before us the goal of "being in full accord and of one mind."

I share this because people are always saying Brethren don't know what we believe. But here, in 1979, the Annual Conference had a good deal to say about what we believe about togetherness without conformity. And this list of what Christian love requires of us is about as central to who we are as Brethren as we can get.

There are loud voices saying that our Brethren style of standing firm where we are but being open to new light is a form of weakness. Harry Truman once called in a group of seven economists for counsel. Each of them had a style of answering that went something like, "On the one hand, thus and so, but on the other hand, it could be thus and so." It is said that Truman became exasperated and shouted, "Will someone please find me a one-armed economist!"

Some people shout for a one-armed doctrine and creed. They don't like any style that says "We affirm this, but on these things we are not agreed." Such a stance is a treasure, particularly for a people who believe that no one has all the light, and that more light may break in at any minute.

Let me give a quick example of how the Brethren style of dealing with conviction and openness, with individual and community conviction, works. My great-grandfather, Jonas Fike, while presiding at a Love Feast, made the mistake of letting the service out early. He was called before the elders, because everyone knew that in the scriptural account, when the upper room events were finished, they "sang a hymn, and went out into the night." So the elders called him before the church for public reprimand and apology.

Now he could have been stubborn and said the community was in the wrong. What he said, according to my dad who was there, was something like this:

> I meant no disrespect to the Scripture. I felt compassion for the farmers who had to get chores done and thought it would be kind to allow them to do them by daylight. I do not believe the Scripture means for us to conform to a Love Feast dismissal time after dark." But then with tears in his eyes, he said, "But if I have offended anyone by my action and brought dishonor to our Lord, I do most sincerely apologize."

In my opinion, that is good Brethren style: the prophetic voice of one standing against the community, but tempering his individuality in submission to the community, even when it was possible that the community might be wrong.

Moses needed help. Strong central leaders cannot do the job alone. Members of the community filled with Spirit power can help. Unchecked individualism is no answer. Yet the community can be wrong in forcing us into conformity.

So here's how I feel about finding the treasure of Brethren togetherness without conformity again. It is, in its own way, as dramatic as a long-lost Mother's Day card.

If we really believe that none of us knows it all, then we will thank God for the witness of brothers and sisters as they share in the community of faith. If we really believe that a whole community of people can be wrong, then we ought to thank God for the individuals who speak out and make us uneasy with new understandings from the Spirit.

If we believe that life is a pilgrimage into maturity, and that revelation is a continuing process, then we ought not be outraged if we have no uniform code for testing and being members of the community.

Finally, if we believe that salvation requires primarily a choice, a commitment to Jesus Christ, then we ought to be grateful that it's possible to conform and be together in our confession of Christ as Lord and at the same time continue to struggle with great diversity on what faithfulness to that confession means.

Such a stance brings us together to listen and learn. It does not allow any of us the right to arm ourselves for covenant shattering confrontation, nor does it allow any of us any secret joy that at last our position has the chance of "winning" in some kind of spiritual combat. Such attitudes have no real foundation in the New Testament or in the best of our tradition. True, we have sometimes separated, but we have done so more often because of rigid personalities than because of theological or biblical issues.

We affirm, but on the other hand we are not agreed. This is togetherness without conformity. Let none of us be tempted to call out for a one-armed theology. The two arms of individual and community will best do the Lord's work with strength and integrity.

16

The Doctor Is Within

2 Kings 5:1-15

The story of Naaman's healing has wonderful characters and an outstanding plot. It features a full-size hero with a problem, a lowly servant girl who wants to help, two kings who could easily start a dangerous political skirmish over the matter, a prophet of the Lord who has the ability to help, and a happy and complete resolution of the hero's problem.

See how quickly the story begins: "Naaman, commander of the army of the king of Aram, was a great man and in high favor with his master because by him the Lord had given victory to Aram. The man, though a mighty warrior, suffered from leprosy."

Here is a man who has position, wealth, and success. He is a victorious commander, a man of valor valued highly by his king, recipient of many honors and awards, liked by his servants, and he has leprosy. That's the first hitch in the story.

Leprosy is not like eczema or poison iv; it is a life-threatening disease. In biblical times, there was no known cure.

What Naaman had ahead of him was an unknown period of deterioration of flesh and limbs. The disease was always progressive, though it advanced at different speeds with different people. Worse yet, the disease ultimately isolated the person from family and friends.

As the story began, Naaman was able to continue his work, but was confined to his home. A lowly Hebrew slave girl, captured and forced into servitude as the maid to Naaman's wife, was touched by the suffering of her master. She mentioned the power of the prophet who resided in Samaria, and wished that her master could see him. When Naaman heard this word, he went to his king for permission to make the visit. The king urged him to go and promised to send along a letter to the King of Israel.

Now comes the second hitch. It's amazing how we tend to believe that all significant things have to be processed through regular channels. When Naaman stood before the king of Israel, with gifts and letter, the king read the message and tore his clothes. "Am I God," he cried, "to give death or life, that this man sends word to me to cure a man of his leprosy?" The King of Aram, he suspected, was trying to pick a quarrel by making an impossible request.

When the prophet Elisha hears about this, he suggested that the King of Israel send Naaman to him. By his intervention, Elisha prevented a dangerous political incident.

Now we come to the third hitch. Naaman went to Elisha with horses, chariots, and full entourage. But Elisha didn't even go out to meet him. Instead, the prophet sent a servant with the message, "Go, and wash in the Jordan seven times, and your flesh shall be restored and you shall be clean."

Naaman was furious. Leper or not, a person of his stature surely deserved more courtesy. Elisha should have waved his wand, and called on the name of the Lord. The rivers of Damascus, he fumed, were cleaner than the muddy Jordan.

Naaman was ready to return to Syria. But his servants said: "Father, if the prophet had commanded you to do something difficult, would you not have done it? How much more, when he all he said to you was, 'Wash, and be clean'?"

This man Naaman had caring servants didn't he? So he washed and found that his illness was cured. He returned to thank Elisha and praise his God. What a great story.

Naaman had an incurable disease. He was suffering and beginning to turn in on himself in despair. How was the cycle broken and his health restored? I believe Naaman changed some things about himself in his submitting to the prophet, and in turn, the power of God was made available to help him to wholeness.

Let's shift the story to a present-day man who had it made. Greg Anderson had his own business and his church growth institute was doing well. He was, in his own mind, using his God-given abilities to do the Lord's work.

Then came the year when a doctor looked him in the eye and said, "Mr. Anderson, the tiger is out of the cage. The cancer that used to be in your lungs has invaded your lymphatic system. Ninety-eight percent of the patients in your condition do not pull through. You may have as little as thirty days. Go home and put your life in order."

Greg Anderson's world collapsed. He said he went through all the classic emotions: guilt; denial, and, most of all, anger. The day after he got the word, he was thinking, "How could God let me die? I'm a good man with a wife and a two-year-old daughter."

In his prayers, he shouted at God: "Take this cancer away. Heal me!"

As he sat there, in pure misery, he said he saw his daughter Erica playing on the floor. "O God," he cried, "I was going to love her so much as she grew up." As if, in some kind of direct answer, the sunlight lit up Erica's golden hair, and three words came into focus in his mind: "Love Erica today."

Not much more profound than, "Go, wash in the Jordan seven times." Yet it made its impact on Greg Anderson. He began to think.

The doctor said ninety-eight percent die. That leaves two percent who live. Maybe if I can find some of those two percent who beat the odds, I can find out how they did it. If they did, maybe I can also.

He began to look and found Mary Doremus in her black wheelchair with a red racing stripe painted on the side. "I hear you have cancer," he said.

"A degenerative illness of the nervous system," she said. "The doctors told me it was fatal. But I'm regaining use of my arms and legs."

"How?" Greg asked.

"I've conquered my illness," she said simply, "and you can too."

"I've already asked God to cure my cancer," Greg said.

"That's a start," Mary told him. "But I didn't say, 'Cure my disease.' I said, 'Conquer it.' That goes much deeper. Instead of asking God to change your physical circumstances, your cancer, you have to ask God to heal you."

Greg said that those words rang true for him. He used to think it was the doctors' responsibility to make him well. Now he knew that this was not true. "It's up to me to be well—emotionally, mentally, spiritually. When God showed me this, it changed my life."

With Mary's help, he also learned another important lesson. "Greg," she said, "your life doesn't change because you live through a serious illness. You live through a serious illness because your life has changed."

In an article four years later titled "Beating the Odds," Greg Anderson reflected that he had come to believe that illness is an invitation to change the focus of life. In Christ, a person can indeed be a new creation.

"We are all going to die," he said. But, "I've come to believe firmly that how long we live is not half as important as how well we live" (story told in *Guideposts,* August 1989).

I want to proceed with special care as we go. Maybe you're wondering about the title of this chapter. I have often sat and looked at the sign that says, "The doctor is in." It's a welcome message when I'm hurting and afraid.

Yet I believe that the stories of Naaman and Greg Anderson tell us that sometimes the doctor is within us. I believe that each of us has inner characteristics that contribute both to our health and to our "dis-ease," or sickness. The doctor is important, so is the doctor within.

Research has shown the close relationship between attitude and health. Positive imaging can contribute to health, while negative imaging can inhibit wholeness and recovery. In *Getting Well Again*, Doctors Simonton and Creighton suggest that all of us participate in becoming sick through a combination of mental, physical, and emotional factors. We may have neglected reasonable diet, exercise, or rest. We may have been tense or anxious for a long period of time without doing enough to relieve the stress. We may have maintained unreasonable workloads or may have tried so hard to meet the needs of others that we neglected ourselves. Perhaps we allowed disappointment or loss to occupy our energy. We may have unduly stretched our physical, emotional and spiritual limits. To the extent that we ignore our limits, these doctors say, we participate in our own illness. They further suggest that when we feel boxed in or trapped by our illness, it is because we are limited by our own beliefs and habitual ways of responding to the illness.

Naaman and Greg Anderson were unwilling to allow themselves to accept their illness in a habitual way. They entered into battle with the circumstance, and changed their lives to help change their situation.

To help with our health and wholeness, we must recognize that the doctor is within our own attitudes and perceptions. And we must do something to aid our own wholeness.

I once read about research suggesting that many illnesses are cured without the victims ever knowing they had them.

As I recall, post-mortem examinations have shown many unmistakable traces of disease that the subjects conquered without knowing it, suggesting our bodies are biased in favor of life rather than death.

Physiologists call this inexorable flow toward wholeness *vis medicatrix naturae,* which simply means "the healing power of nature." Scar a tree with an ax, and when you return, you see the healing. Cut your finger peeling peaches, as my wife Jean did the other day, and with a little antiseptic and a band aid, something else works the healing. Galen, a physician who lived in Rome around A.D. 164, said, "I dressed the wound, but God did the healing." I believe that God-given bias toward health is a doctor within each of us.

In his book *Health and Healing,* Andrew Weil, M.D., says that in our society the commonality of religion and medicine is obscured. Too often medical doctors pay attention only to the physical. As a result they do not see or integrate nonphysical forces that animate and direct the physical body.

"Science and intellect can show us mechanisms and details of physical reality," Weil notes, "and that knowledge is surely of value." But they cannot unveil the deep mysteries of the integrated relationship between spirit and body. Current research shows that those who have a meaningful religious life are healthier than those who do not.

This tells us that the contribution we make toward our own health is not only in our attitudes and lifestyle, but also in our spiritual well-being. The spirit can be healthy and at peace while the body is sick. If the spirit is healthy, the process of healing is encouraged.

Harold S. Kushner's book *When Bad Things Happen to Good People* has blessed many of us. In the book, he tells the story of Martin Gray, a survivor of the Warsaw Ghetto.

After the Holocaust, Gray rebuilt his life and became successful. He married and raised a family. Life again seemed good. Then one day his wife and family were killed when a forest fire raged through their home in southern France.

Gray was distraught, pushed to the limit by this added tragedy. People urged him to demand an inquiry into what caused the fire. But as he lived through this hell, he came to see that an investigation would focus only on the past, on the issues of pain, sorrow, and blame. He wanted to focus on the future.

Further, he saw, an inquiry would set him against other people. And he felt that accusing other people of being responsible for your misery only makes the loneliness more miserable.

"Life," he said, "has to be lived for something, not just against something."

A simple yet powerful idea. It sounds a little like Greg Anderson hearing the words, "Love Erica today." It also sounds like Naaman's servants suggesting that if he were asked to do some great thing he would do it, so why not some simple thing.

Why not some simple thing for us? Some simple thing like realizing that if life is lived for something rather than against something, the focus of life is changed. Some simple thing like realizing that healing may be different from being cured. Some simple thing like unashamedly allowing God's healing spirit, the doctor that is within us, to have a significant place in our lives. Some simple yet difficult thing such as being responsible for our own lives in such a way that we contribute to our wholeness rather than our dis-ease.

The simple is not always easy, but it is never complicated.

Writing in *Pulpit Digest* (July/Aug. 1989), Edward Paul Cohn gives us both caution and encouragement: "We dare not be simplistic," he tells us. "Positive thinking is no cure, but despair and hopelessness is too high a price for anyone to pay who must wage war with sickness!

"You are what you think," he continues, "either a helpless victim consigned to a jail of despair, or one who has the nerve to summon the resources of inner courage and raw faith in defiance of life-threatening despair or sickness."

French workers used to wear wooden shoes called *sabots.* When the workers felt abused by those who owned the factory in which they worked, they would retaliate by throwing their sabots into the machinery, thus stopping, or sabotaging, the works.

There is a doctor within us. We sabotage our own lives by throwing into our minds messages of negativism and defeat, messages of anger and despair, messages of self indulgence which jam us up so that the resources available to help us to wholeness don't have a chance.

When Robert Louis Stevenson was coughing out his life with a lung disease, his wife, Fanny, walked into the bedroom and said, "Well, I suppose you'll tell me that it's a glorious day."

"Yes," the noted author replied, looking at the sunlight streaming through his window, "I refuse to let a row of medicine bottles be my horizon" (quoted in *Pulpit Resource,* vol. 17, no. 3, 1989, p. 24). He may not have been cured, but he was healed.

If we were asked to do some difficult thing to cure a life-threatening or unhealthy situation, wouldn't we do it? Why not some simple thing, like Naaman or Greg Anderson did? Some simple thing like opening ourselves to be healed even if we aren't cured. Such a simple thing will help turn the doctor within us loose for battle and thereby give us a shot at new life.

17

A Quiet Place
Mark 6:30-34, 53-56; Ps. 23

A friend of mine, with tongue in cheek, told his congregation that a miracle had happened in day camp during the past week. The miracle, he said, "was that seventeen first graders were lined up along Conewago Creek fishing, and not one of them ended up with a hook in the scalp or cheek!"

Pretty amazing when you think of it. But let me propose a different possible miracle, the miracle of coming home from vacation really rested and ready to go! Wouldn't that be a switch for most of us?

Isn't it ironic that we are so energized to get away from it all that our vacations are almost as compulsive, as fretful, as schedule bound as our normal lives? We want so badly for our vacation to include all the things that we want to do and see, that we try to do too much and end up unrested, tired, and unrenewed. I'm reminded of a prospectus from a Swiss hotel which read: "This place is known as the perfect resort for those wanting solitude. People searching for solitude are, in fact, flocking here from all corners of the globe."

There is no doubt that we all need vacations. We not only need vacations from work, we need a respite from the clutter and busyness and noise of everyday life. We talk about a vacation as getting away from it all. But that's hard to do.

The beach used to be a getaway place, where the loudest noise was the surf and the delighted screams of bathers as they tested the temperature of the water. Now one can scarcely hear any of those wonderful relaxing sounds because of the sound of boom boxes turned up to indescribable decibels. When I walk each day, I often see other walkers and joggers. Maybe half of them are wearing earphones with tape recorders or CD players.

Walking can be a wonderful quiet time filled with birdsong, the rustle of wind, the sound of water. You can sort through ideas and thoughts you don't otherwise have time to think about. But those exercisers choose to fill their quiet time with manufactured sounds they can hear anytime.

We used to live across the street from a men's dorm at a college. In the fall, that colorful and softly peaceful time of year when you can have the windows up and enjoy the left-over warmth before the cold sets in, the residents would throw up their windows, put their one hundred watt stereos on the window sill, and blast their music out into the autumn tranquility.

What's more, each window had its own music and no one seemed to mind that all of it together created a monstrous cacophony. Darkness proved no hindrance to the concerts. Into the wee hours, our houses and senses were bombarded.

In my more peevish moments, I thought about repaying their concert with one of my own. Perhaps I could place my stereo outside on the patio at six o'clock Sunday morning, turn my speakers toward their open windows and play the *1812 Overture* as loud as my equipment could manage.

But one insensitivity does not deserve another, and besides, Sunday morning is a wonderfully quiet time on campus. Also, it would have been a shame to disturb the wonderful mockingbird who often created its own early morning variations on a hundred themes.

Quiet time is a blessing that we seem to have misplaced. As someone has said,

Substitutes for repose are a billion dollar business. Almost daily, new antidotes for contemplation spring into being and leap out from store counters. Silence, already the world's most critical shortage, is almost a nasty word. Modern people may or may not be obsolete, but they are certainly wired for sound and they twitch as naturally as they breathe. (*Pulpit Resource*, vol. X, no. 3, p. 11)

The Bible understood the need for us to come away to a quiet place. In the creation story itself, there was a day of rest. But we've decided putting a little weekend in our life is something we should work at with frenzy. So weekends are not quiet, restful times—they are times to do as much as we can of what we are otherwise too busy to do.

In Mark 6, Jesus suggested a clue to a more healthy and whole life. The apostles have just returned from traveling through the villages, healing and teaching. They were probably still riding on an adrenaline high, bubbling with excitement and delight in what they had been doing.

But as they were reporting to Jesus, there was so much going on around them with people coming and going that there was little time for conversation. So Jesus said, "Come away to a deserted place all by yourselves and rest a while."

They got into a boat to go to a different location. But the rest doesn't last for long. A crowd of people followed them, and the account moved immediately into the feeding the five thousand.

We'll not make the normal move to the hungry crowd. For now, let's pause and consider Jesus' invitation to come to a quiet place.

There is a certain sense of relief for me in this passage. Jesus and his followers are doing important lifesaving work. Yet he advises them, "Come away to a deserted place."

Everyone needs a quiet place—even the Savior of the world. This should help us to deal with whatever pangs of guilt we may experience in finding a quiet place for ourselves.

Let's clarify a difference in quiet places. Richard Foster, in his book *The Celebration of Discipline,* makes a helpful distinction between isolation and solitude. Isolation is usually inflicted upon us by circumstance; solitude is freely chosen. Isolation is negative aloneness; solitude is positive aloneness. Loneliness is inner emptiness; solitude is inner fulfillment.

Choosing to be in a quiet place is different from being forced to be alone. Solitude is controlled by our desire for it, by our making time for it. Isolation may be the product of a job (as a lighthouse keeper or a scientist at an Arctic weather station). Or isolation can be the aftermath of broken relationships (whether caused by divorce, death, or disagreement). Jesus invites us to solitude, not isolation.

A recent TV news segment reported on the growing popularity of spending vacations or retreat times in centers that focus on spiritual and personal renewal. People confessed that silence and contemplation were experiences that renewed and invigorated them.

I suspect that we are created with a craving for solitude. Isn't one of the many things we like about the Twenty-third Psalm the reference to still waters and the connection of this image to the restoration of our souls? The need for a quiet place is inherent in our being. If we don't feel it, it's because we have unlearned it.

I am not an avid or expert photographer. But like most families, we have a treasure of pictures. One that Jean and I often speak of is a picture of our older son, Joe, then a city kid about ten years of age. In the photo, he is lying on the bank at his grandmother's house in rural Virginia, hands behind his head, a stalk of rye grass in his teeth. We noticed him there for perhaps for an hour, doing nothing. No, not doing nothing—doing something he had trouble finding time or place to do in the city.

Do you remember seeking solitude as a child? Did you ever build caves with chairs and blankets to hide under and be by yourself? Did you ever have some little corner of the house that you used to go to when you wanted to be alone? If you didn't have one of your own, did you ever envy the friend who had a private tree house?

Some of my most vivid memories are of quiet times alone, lying flat on my back in a wheat field waiting for the wagon to come from the barn to be loaded. I was resting physically but noticing the blue sky, the green trees, the golden wheat, and feeling the warm sun. I recall kneeling by my bedroom window in the wee hours of the morning, watching and listening to a vicious thunderstorm crack and roll.

I believe that as children, most of us knew the value of a quiet place alone. That's one of the childish things we shouldn't have put away when we grew up. We were healthier and more whole with it.

Solitude gives us a chance to think. The painter Grant Wood once said, "All the really good ideas I ever had came to me while I was milking a cow."

So much of what we do requires attention that we don't have time to think. In the old days people in a buggy or wagon could let their minds wander, but it's dangerous in an auto on a daily commute.

Solitude gives us a chance to ask questions we might not otherwise ask. We hear a lot of criticism about the violence of electronic games. In a moment of solitude one time, I asked myself whether the energy expended in competitive destruction in such games might be transferred to competitive service. Why not develop an electronic game in which you electronically see how much of the world's available food resources could be distributed to the hungry in the least amount of time? The one who served the most, avoided all the political pitfalls, used the resources most wisely, and met the most needs would be the winner. Nothing will every come of that idea, but it's one that I wouldn't have had time to think about without a little solitude.

Solitude also gives us a chance to be confronted by the reality of God. Alfred North Whitehead defined religion as that which a person does with his or her solitude. Solitude gives us a chance to let God work in our consciousness.

Sometimes we do not want solitude. Noise becomes an avoidance syndrome for us.

At one time I was impressed by the theory that the brain could do much more than we ask it to do, possibly even do more than one thing at a time. I think I still agree with that. But to believe that students can do their best, most creative work on school assignments while watching TV strains my credulity. I suspect the insistence on watching and working is really an effort to avoid concentrated working. That is, sometimes we do not want solitude because it forces us to face something we don't want to face.

One of the forms of punishment sometimes used is forced aloneness, such as when my daughter sent our granddaughter to her bedroom for a "time out" until she straightened out. I remember times when I was instructed to sit in the corner and not come out until I would apologize and mean it. Those were quiet times of painful reflection. But in the quiet, I had a chance to rethink and weigh the issues. I had a chance to blame others, to feel wronged and sorry for myself. Yet finally, I could work through the issues and own my part of what happened. I could think about what might be necessary to get out of the corner and on with life.

Sometimes we resist quiet time for the very reason we should covet it. It gives us a chance to be confronted by God—to let the reality of God's way come upon us.

Last, solitude gives us a chance to review and renew. Energy is more than physical. We physically rest when we sleep, and that's a real blessing. But if we awake tired before we start the day, that's not physical—that's emotional and spiritual fatigue.

We need to learn to take time to ponder what we are doing, how we are doing it, and why we are doing it. We need time to renew our commitment, to think how we might better accomplish what we want to do, or time to simply rest from the demands of what we are doing. This grace is available if we heed the invitation of Jesus to "come away."

A quiet place is not something someone gives to us—it's something we choose to take. It's not something denied us by others—it's something we allow others to deny us.

There is a little known story in 1 Kings 20 about a guard who was asked to take charge of a prisoner. When he failed in his task and lost the prisoner, he said to the king, "While your servant was busy here and there, he was gone."

We've been given charge of our lives, and a place of solitude is important to the health and wholeness of us all. If it's gotten away from us, it's because we've been so busy with this and that, that it escaped.

Heed the advice of Jesus. Come with him to a quiet place. It could be in the wakeful hours of the night. It could be in your backyard or on a porch rocker, during a short stroll or in taking a few minutes to watch a sunset. It could be anywhere, but for it to be somewhere, sometime, you must take the initiative.

18

The Aggravating Loss of Niceness

Rom. 12:9-21

It was early morning in Chicago, sometime in 1959. Our church and the attached parsonage in which our family lived was located at the corner of Congress Parkway and Central Park. There was a traffic light on the corner, and many people tried to race through after the light changed.

On this particular morning, Jean and I heard sirens. That was not unusual in itself. But these didn't race on by. They seemed at the other end of our bedroom. We dressed quickly and rushed out.

There on the corner were the rescue squad, the fire truck, the long hook and ladder truck, the fire chief, and several police officers. All of this for a little fender bender between two cars, one trying to dash through at the last millisecond of the yellow light and the other trying to race through at the first flash of green. Jean raised the obvious question: Why all this equipment for such a little event?

Romans 12 may seem a little like that. Here we are in the midst of God's salvation symphony, and we come to this little chapter. Somehow it seems bland by comparison with the booming percussion of civil authority issues in Romans 13 and like a forgettable air on the flute when set over against the full orchestra crescendos of Romans 8.

Don't get me wrong. I'm not demeaning what is here. I am simply indicating that at first glance it seems to be less demanding, less profound, than most of the other passages in the letter to the Christians in Rome. In a way, the passage seems to be saying, "Be nice to one another."

Is such a message worthy of our deeper inspection? Let me put it another way. Have you noticed the kind of aggravating loss of niceness in our society?

Leo Durocher, the famous Brooklyn Dodger manager, is credited with coining the phrase "nice guys finish last." This seems to be a growing philosophy.

In Atlanta, an angry shopper hurled a box of shoes at a clerk and stalked out the door. In New York, two elderly women were spun out of a revolving door and thrown across the lobby of an apartment building by younger people in a hurry. In Los Angeles a woman at the end of a line, waited at the Bureau of Motor Vehicles for forty-five minutes, only to have the clerk slam the window in her face.

I once clipped a letter a man wrote a letter to the editor of a local paper about standing in line for a theater ticket and hearing the conversation of two teenage girls in the line behind him: "Their talk was generously sprinkled with scatological monosyllables for excrement and the sex act. It was like standing in the dull blue haze of someone else's tobacco smoke."

We live in a time of rudeness and insensitivity. I suspect that you've had your own experiences with rudeness or anger, perhaps while shopping, waiting in the checkout line at the grocery, standing at an airline counter, trying to study in the library, or seeing the latest example of road rage. There really seems to be an aggravating loss of niceness. Perhaps Romans 12 can help us in some recovery or renewal.

We are not born into niceness. Politeness and respect for others are learned behaviors. Being nice is a cultivated virtue.

It does not come automatically, either by birth or through baptism into the body of Christ. Jesus spent a great deal of time talking about people who were good but not necessarily nice—people like the scribes and pharisees—good men, religious men, faithful men, but not so nice.

In your congregation, you will be obliged to relate to good people who know how to be insensitive and abrasive. Politeness and respect for others are learned behaviors.

Here's a little piece of dialogue from my early home life. My mother is speaking.

"Earle Jr., did you wash your hands before coming to the table?"

"Yes."

"Yes what?"

"Yes, ma'am."

It was not a game. It was a serious part of my early training. The only way to avoid the question was to do it right the first time.

In those days, a child did not address any adult without adding ma'am or sir. I've long since lost that. And I seldom hear it from young people today. But once in a while, when it happens, it's nice.

Norman Vincent Peale once said that his mother "always cautioned us children whenever we were invited somewhere to eat to 'mind our manners.'" His minister father used to protest that she seemed to place manners on a par with morals. "Not so," she said, "but your morals aren't always showing. Your manners are."

Being nice is not easy. Paul said:

Love one another with mutual affection; outdo one another in showing honor. . . . Contribute to the needs of the saints; extend hospitality to strangers. Bless those who persecute you; bless and do not curse them. Rejoice with those who rejoice, weep with those who weep. Live in harmony with one another; do not be haughty but associate with the lowly; do not claim to be wiser than you are. Do not repay anyone evil for evil, but take thought for what is noble in the sight of all. If it is possible, so far as it depends on you, live peaceably with all. Beloved, never avenge yourselves, but leave room for the wrath of God. . . . Do not be overcome by evil, but overcome evil with good.

Reviewing that list reveals that being nice to one another is not a biblical snack at a fast food drive through—it's a full course meal, and it smacks of hard work.

Maybe that's why we avoid being nice—it's difficult. Or maybe we think it's weak to be polite, to be courteous, to be respectful. After all, nice people finish last, or as Robert J. Winger implied in his book *Winning Through Intimidation,* you can only be successful if you are willing to force the other person to take some initiative against you. If you intimidate them, nine times out of ten, they won't challenge you. Hence, niceness is weakness which the strong take advantage of to gain their way.

That principle was put into effect by a proprietor of chain stores on the West Coast. He trained workers that whenever a customer asked for a pack of gum, the clerk was to lay two packs on the counter. The reason? Chances are the customer would buy two, because it takes less time to pay than to challenge the clerk. Most customers opt to avoid confrontation. Thus, the discourteous turn out to be the strong, and the nice person is taken advantage of.

None of us wants to be a patsy. Yet it is possible to be polite but firm in not buying two items when we ask for only one. One doesn't need to make a loud speech about salespersons being hard of hearing or to give a lecture on the ethics of manipulation through intimidation. One has only to say, "No, I only wanted one." And that can be done nicely.

We can deal in a similar way with telemarketers who bombard us with calls we don't want to receive. We can politely say, "I'm sorry, I'm not interested," and hang up while they go on with their spiel.

We should not be seduced by the "how to succeed" gurus of our day. Intimidation is not required to be successful, and it is certainly not a virtue worth cultivating.

But alternatives Paul lists are hard. Overcoming the evil of intimidation with good is not easy. It's easier to be nasty.

Or perhaps we have succumbed to the popular belief that it is harmful to squelch anger. Let it all hang out, we've been counseled. Pent-up hostility is harmful, and we should be open and honest with our feelings.

Yet honesty about our anger does not require the destruction of another person. Being clear about our own feelings does not necessitate rudeness to another, not even toward the person who makes us angry. Niceness is hard work. It requires control, not denial.

That grand old Chicago minister of bygone days, Preston Bradley, was a golfer. Actually, he was a hacker like most of us. He regularly played with some of his parishioners who marveled at the fact that they never heard him shout, fuss, throw things, or curse at his performance.

One of his playing partners asked him one day how he managed to play with such self control. He responded: "You have perhaps noticed that after each bungling effort I pause and spit. You will find that where that spit falls, the grass will not grow for a year."

That's honesty about anger without needing to lash out at someone else for talking or distracting you when you play. Anger in itself is not evil. How we manage it is what makes it awful or acceptable.

While there are myriad excuses for not being nice, there is really no acceptable reason for it. Our salvation is not at stake in our attempts to follow Paul's list of ways to be nicer, but our witness and enjoyment are.

This is not an impossible list, not nearly so difficult as taking up our cross and following Jesus, losing our life to find it, or selling all we have and giving it to the poor. There isn't a single thing listed here that each one of us is not able to do if we make the effort.

I enjoy Robert Fulghum's writings. In his book *It Was on Fire When I Lay Down on It,* he tells of sitting in the Hong Kong airport beside a young woman. Everything about her said "young American student going home." The backpack beside her bore the scars and dirt of hard traveling. Let me share the experience in Fulghum's words:

> When the tears began to drip from your chin I imagined some lost love, or the sorrow of giving up adventure for college classes. But when you began to shake with sobs, you drew me into your sadness. A good cry seemed in order, and weep you did . . . all over me. My handkerchief, your handkerchief, most of a small box of tissues and both your sleeves were needed to dry up the flood before you finally got it out. . . . your plane was about to go and you had lost your ticket.

Folghum continues:

> After we dried you off, I and a nice older couple from Chicago who were also swept away in the tide of your tears, offered to take you to lunch and to talk to the powers that be at the airlines about some remedy. You stood up to go with us, turned around to pick up your belongings and SCREAMED! I thought you had been shot. But no . . . it was your ticket. You had found your ticket. You had been sitting on it for three hours.

Folghum concludes:

> Like a sinner saved from the jaws of hell, you laughed and cried and hugged us all and suddenly you were gone

. . . leaving most of the passenger lounge limp from being part of your drama. And now often when I am sitting on my own ticket in some way; sitting on whatever it is I have that will get me up and on to what comes next, I think of you.

Amid the aggravating loss of niceness time in today's world, here are some words to remember: "Love one another with mutual affection; outdo one another in showing honor. . . . Contribute to the needs of the saints; extend hospitality to strangers. . . . Do not repay anyone evil for evil, but take thought for what is noble in the sight of all. . . . Do not be overcome by evil, but overcome evil with good.

That's our ticket for not being conformed to this world but being transformed by the renewal of our mind and will. There isn't a one of us who can't do this—at least if we don't sit on it.

19

A Warm Finger
for a Frosty Pane

Isa. 63:7-9; John 3:16

This grouchy gloomy man is seated in a diner consuming coffee and a donut while he reads the morning paper. He is obviously in bad sorts, so the little waitress, thinking to put a different perspective on his feelings, smiled at him when he paid his bill, thanked him brightly, and added, "Have a nice day!" The man scowled at her and said abruptly, "I had something else in mind, thank you!"

It may be a hard time right now for you to have a nice day. A family situation may wear heavy on your spirit. Living every day in a climate of domestic and international violence may serve to whither your cheerful quotient. Pain or poor health may be daily fare for you. Disappointment in a loved one or yourself may make optimism hard to come by. Loneliness or sorrow in the loss of a loved one may make the character of your days less than "clear and sunny." Whether occasional or regular, there are times when someone says, "Have a nice day," and we feel like saying, "I had something else in mind."

Some years back, a picture on the front of a Sunday bulletin caught my eye. It had a kind of "have a nice day" feel to it which wouldn't allow me to give a disgruntled response. It was the picture of a window pane which bitter cold had so frosted that it was impossible to see anything through the window. But a warm finger had written the word *LOVE* right across the frost. The heat from the finger had melted the frost, and what before had been an opaque pane, now provided a message that could be read, and if you stood close enough, you could see through the message of love to the world outside.

Maybe for some of you, it seems a stretch to see hope in such a simple picture. Maybe for some it seems forced to see a sign of warmth amid frost. But not for me. Something in me refuses to say that the confusion, the despair, the problems, the fears, the unknowns are the last words for this day or the days which are yet in front of us. Something in me looks for, believes in, and rejoices in the possibility of a warm finger on a frosty pane to set the tone, the character, the perspective for life. Let me see if I can help you do the same.

The Israelites had a way of wringing hope out of the almost completely dry fabric of a lament. In fact, that should not surprise us. Hope, in its inherent meaning, would not be necessary if everything were perfect. We do not hope for the worst, we hope for the best. We do not hope that things will fall to pieces, we hope for things to get better. Hope, as an emotion or feeling, has no place except where there are problems. One does not hope for things one already has. We hope for the unseen, the unpossessed, the unpresent. We hope for that which is missing. We hope for anything which will make it better.

This short text from Isaiah 63 is the beginning of an intercessory prayer for the people. It is a lamentation. Form critics would tell us to look for four parts: (1) recital of past blessing, (2) description of present need, (3) appeal for help, and (4) assurance that the prayer will be heard. This particular text works only at the recital of past blessings. And a part of its importance is its attention to the meaning of memory.

The Hebrew word *za-kair* is used in the causative tense, meaning, "I will cause you to remember." Israel understood that in the remembering, there was both hope and redemption. Memory is connected with action—action received and action taken. Memory calls us to thanksgiving, repentance, and reaching out to God. Even during the exile (which was over by the time this part of Isaiah was written), even amid adversity and despair, the memory of whose they were and the memory of past blessings could bring the Israelite out of despair into hope, out of depression into eager joy. Israel understood that reality. Is there something we can learn from them? Is there a warm finger for a frosty day we have trouble calling nice?

I read of a psychiatrist in New York city named John Rosen, who worked with catatonic patients. He broke all precedents doctors have of remaining separate and aloof from their patients. He moved into the ward with them. He placed his bed among their beds. He lived the life they must live. Day-to-day, he shared it. If they didn't talk, he didnt talk either. It's as if he understood what was happening. He was just there, and that communicated something to them that they hadn't felt in years. Somebody understood.

But then he did something else. He put his arms around them and hugged them. This M.D., PhD, this highly skilled, highly paid physician, held these unattractive, stiff, unresponsive, unlovable, incontinent persons and warmed them with the strong arms of his caring. Often when they came back to life, when they first spoke, the first thing they said to him was "thank you."

Amid being almost immobilized by circumstance and environment, amid catatonic confusion and catastrophic uncertainty, amid fear and a strong grouchy feeling that we had something else in mind than having a nice day, God can, in the gift of Jesus Christ, put strong arms of love around us and hold us, and bring us back to life. In Christ, God's finger writes love on the cold of all the world's pain. And if we see it, we can also see through it with hope and with anticipation.

I'm not speaking of unrealistic joy, false exuberance. I think of this as a return to wholeness, the recovery of a perspective which is able to say, despite what happens, "Thank you God for being with us in this way. Thank you for the warmth of love amid cold. Thank you for writing your mark on the world in your son, Jesus Christ. Thank you for the finger of love that leaves its warm message where we can see it and see through it."

Now, it would be presumptuous to assume that everyone will say a hearty "Amen." For some, I'm sure, there is a nagging little notion that creates a contrapuntal melody under such a confession. "Too easy . . . Too easy!" And then the fugue gets expanded by thoughts like, "I don't get it. I can't see the warm finger, nor can I see through the frost. Either it's not there or I don't know the right formula."

But the reality is, there is no set formula, no special gift which one has over another into getting from the grouches to some sense of joy. Though I consider myself grown up, I still like to get toys. This year my sister gave me a toy Porsche that runs by battery and electronic controls. I like it. Several years ago, I received an electronic "Master Mind" game. If you don't know how it works, let me describe it. When you play by yourself, as you turn it on, you choose the difficulty you want to work against, that is, three, four, or five unknown digits locked into the little computer's memory. By guessing the numbers in sequence, and being told with each guess how many numbers you have right, and how many are in the right sequence, you are supposed to, by deduction, come up with the right numbers in the right sequence. When you make your final guess, and it is correct, the little machine blinks approval and tells you how many times it took you to get the right answer.

A warm finger for the frosty pane of life is not some kind of divine master-mind game which God plays with us. It is not a complicated process of trial and error deduction. There is not some secret formula which, when you're smart enough to work through it, will blink its approval in some newfound sense of enthusiasm and joy. God's presence in the world is there if we want to see it and see through it.

Still, if we really feel like the man at the coffee counter, having a pastor tell us God's gift of love and warmth is with us won't necessarily change our mood. Maybe something in the Hebrew process of remembering might help.

Try this! What one or two people are most important to you? Would you want to be without them? Is your life blessed by them? Is that not worth noting? Is that not a past blessing? Is that not a remembrance of past blessing which gives hope and joy for tomorrow? Is that not some equivalent of a warm finger on whatever frost clouds your life?

Or try the remembering exercise in another way. If you were asked to list three things that are most important to you right now in your life, what would they be? Now having listed them, suppose some arbitrary power would make you choose the one you would be most willing to give up. Would the loss of one negate the continued blessing of the other two? You would not be asked to deny the pain of losing one of the three, but could you feel any joy at having two blessings left? Could the remembering of two blessings provide hope and joy for the future? Can any sub-zero frost take away that which you rejoice in having?

Why must we have our joy Simon-pure? Why is it that we are only willing to call it joy if its on our terms? Why is it, that faced with today and tomorrow, we allow a cloud here and a setback there, some major reversal or loss, to set the tone for this day and for those days which are still in front of us? Why can't we have "nice day" feelings amid catastrophic pain or heartbreak. The frost may be there, but so can the mark of the warm finger.

I believe any one of us can remember, in the Hebrew understanding of the word. I believe that any of us can see the warm finger of God at work in the world. Is there any way that your life is blessed at all? In that blessing, God is trying to speak to you. Are you loved at all, by anyone? In that love, God is trying to speak to you about love. Is there anything you can do well? In that gift God is speaking to you about joy and meaning in life. Does anyone really care about you? In that care, God is putting a warm finger on the frost of life for your benefit.

You remember the fable of Chanticleer, the rooster. Being a vain sort, he prided himself on his accomplishments. Most of all, he congratulated himself for the sun rise, for as anyone could observe, his crowing each morning caused the sun to appear on the horizon. Invariably, it happened. But one morning, Chanticleer overslept. When he awoke, he was surprised and chagrined. There was the sun high in the sky, and it had gotten there without one little peep from him. Thinking things over, he realized that he could not honestly take credit for causing the sun to rise. But he said, "If by my crowing I cannot bring in the dawn, then by my crowing, I can celebrate its coming."

There is not some mysterious formula, some special characteristic which allows some persons to look at this day and the days which are ahead with joy. All it take is some honesty that realizes that being blessed is not something that we bring about by our faith or our crowing. It is not generated by spiritual muscles. But having a nice day is somehow related to remembering how our lives have already been blessed, and recognizing blessings as they come.

There is a warm finger of love God initiated in the frosty world in which you and I live. If we will receive it, feel its strength around us, confess it, and let it be what it is, we may indeed look at the blessings of this day and look through the love of God to those days which are ahead of us with some sense of optimism, some sense of hope, some sense of gratitude. O yes, one final thing. Have a nice day!

20

On the Up and Up
Isa. 2:1-5; Ps. 122:1-4

Good Housekeeping magazine carried a cartoon in which a proud waiter was shown carrying a platter through a restaurant full of diners. The entree on the platter looked like a Halloween jack-o'-lantern with turkey drumsticks attached, all topped off with a jaunty Santa Claus hat. A lady diner was saying to her escort: "I guess it really is true. The holidays are running together."

Today is the first Sunday of Advent. But it's hard to feel we're poised at the start of a significant season when the stack of Christmas catalogues has been getting higher and higher since early September. The commercial world has put the cart before the horse. The wagon load of season trappings somehow moves ahead of the power of the good news, which should pull us into the celebration of this season.

This week, a newspaper columnist reminded us that, on the first Sunday of Advent, those of us who are Christians might well wish each other a Happy New Year. For the church, Advent is the beginning of the Christian year. It is a promise of all that is to come. It is a time of anticipation, a time of expectation.

So, how would the expectation of Advent stack up against the expectation for the beginning of deer season? For some of us, it's no contest. But suppose there were a spiritual meter that measured a person's level of Advent anticipation, on a scale of minus fifty to plus fifty. Suppose you were required, on this first Sunday of Advent, to touch an electronic pad in front of you to register your Advent enthusiasm. What would the meter show? Would the reading be high or low, up or down?

A few people might register a zero; which would show they don't care much either way. All the descendants of Scrooge would be in the minus department. Some hearty souls whose spiritual prowess puts the rest of us to shame might register on the high end of the plus scale.

My hunch is that most of us would register a mixed reading. If there were a place on the meter for ambivalence, a range of feelings that are somehow up and down at the same time, that's probably where our readings would come out.

Wherever you think your reading would register, do you wish it were different? Would you like to be more up for advent than you are?

I confess to a kind of annual ambivalence at Advent. I experience down feelings that make me feel tired before it starts, frazzled feelings that come from a calendar cluttered with important and unnecessary things I'm expected to do, and usually some almost hostile feelings that the weight of commercialism tarnishes and diminishes the deeper intention of the promise of God's good news. But there are also positive feelings related to eagerness for the great music of the season, anticipation of sharing time and traditions with loved ones, eagerness to relive the Christmas Word in significant times of worship, and anticipation of the chance to share in the joy and happiness of children.

One strategy to deal with such ambivalence is to name it, recognize that we have some control over it, and make a conscious effort to get up for the season. As I struggled with my Advent meter reading for this year, I decided that I not only wanted to be up to celebrating this season—that is, somehow able to live above the cultural commercial pressures which I can do very little about—but I also felt a real tug in my soul to be on the up and up. That is, I wanted to go beyond being above the commercialization on up to experiencing the high meaning of the promise of God's Christmas gift.

Maybe what pushed me there was a question someone asked: "Do you feel like you are getting ready for a holiday or a holy day?" Something in me knew the answer was that I would surely like to be getting ready for a holy day. If anything in you longs for this season to be just a little more than normal, just a little higher on the scale of significance, a little more on the up, then let's look more closely at the text from Isaiah 2.

To be sure, Isaiah isn't a Christmas text in and of itself. There are familiar verses in this book that are dear to those of us in the peace church heritage. But these verses are often used as an Advent text because they have in them the Old Testament equivalent of Advent expectation. The vision of what the kingdom of God would be like is wrapped up in the coming of the Messiah, the advent of God's anointed presence in the world. And that's what the Gospels understand the advent of Jesus to be. What you must do is hold in your mind the parallel understanding of the Old Testament coming of the kingdom and the New Testament understanding of the coming of the incarnate God in Christ Jesus.

The anticipation and expectation quotient is high in Isaiah 2:1-5. The prophet offered vivid imagery that may be helpful to us in our contemporary Advent preparation. "In days to come the mountain of the Lord's house shall be established as the highest of mountains," verse two says, and so "All the nations shall stream to it."

In *Exegetical Resource* (vol. 20, no. 4, p. 27) Charles Wolfe says we should ask questions of this passage that a five-year-old might ask. That is, "Why the highest mountain, and how can nations stream to the highest mountain? Things don't flow uphill."

It's not a mistranslation. The text indicates that the mountain of the Lord is the chief mountain. It is the head mountain, therefore the tallest one, lifted above all others. And all the people of the world will flow toward it. The verb is the one used for liquids and comes from the same root as river.

The point is that even though God is high and lifted up, the one above all others, people will be drawn to God. As naturally as the power of gravity makes the river flow, as mysteriously and supernaturally as moving against the tide, people will flow toward God.

The flowing up to the Lord is not compelled. People are not captive to some overpowering force. Rather, they are attracted. There is a positive choice to flow in this direction: "Many peoples shall come and say, 'Come, let us go up to the mountain of the Lord.'"

To flow in that direction is an invitation we can respond to or ignore. In the text there is Advent feeling; there is eagerness, expectation, anticipation: "Come, let us go. . . ."

The motivation for all of this is also clear. The people want to go up so God "may teach us his ways and that we may walk in his paths." When that happens, when we walk in the path of the Lord, there is the promise of transformation. Swords will be beaten into plowshares and spears into pruning hooks. Not only are the weapons disabled, they are put to constructive use. Nations will not learn war anymore.

Doesn't something in you yearn for such a day to come? Isn't something in you drawn toward that high vision of a peaceful kingdom even though your scientific and practical self tells you that the world as you know it either can't or won't flow uphill to that kind of ideal?

But what if it could? What if it would? Would you want it if it were possible? Would you be excited about it? Would you look forward to it? If there is even a little tiny yes murmuring in your soul, you have an intuition as to what Advent is about. You are on your way to the upside of the season.

But there's more. There's a final invitation in verse five: "O house of Jacob, come, let us walk in the light of the Lord!" Which is to say, when we hear the invitation to go up to the mountain of the Lord, and when we learn about the ways of the Lord, then we are to walk in those ways.

The transformation requires our full participation. We are to be on the way up in our going, but if we want to be on the up-and-up side of Advent, we need to be willing to walk in the ways in which we are taught. The vision is not accomplished against our defenses or by magnetic attraction, but through our eager participation, our willingness to walk in the light.

Have you been keeping the New Testament gift of God in a parallel column in your mind? Do you remember how John's gospel describes that gift? It is described there as light coming into the world, and as such, a light that darkness cannot overcome.

"Come, house of Jacob," the Isaiah passage says, "let us walk in the light and be in the advent of the kingdom." "Come body of Christ," John's gospel says, "let us walk in the light and be in the advent of God's coming into the world. Come struggling weary Christians; come too busy disciples; come all who wish to get ready for a holy day rather than just a holiday. Come let us go up to the mountain and take one step more upwards and walk in the light of Advent."

I hear your question, "How? Even when I want to flow upstream, even when I feel the tug to let this Advent be more up than down, even if I might dare to hope that my advent might be on the up-and-up, how can I?" Let's talk about that in two ways, from an outer and an inner perspective.

What are some outward visible things we might do for Advent to be on the up and up? Jo Robinson and Jean Coppock Staeheli have co-authored a helpful book entitled *Unplug the Christmas Machine*. They suggest some things we might try in an effort to live above the commercial quagmires of the season:

- try to be a peacemaker, within your family and community;
- take intentional time to enjoy being with your family;
- create a beautiful home environment for the season;
- make intentional time to celebrate the birth of Jesus;
- seek out some way to help persons less fortunate;
- strengthen or mend bonds with relatives;
- intentionally make time to relax and be renewed.

On the surface, these suggestions might seem like just a lot more to do. But there's merit in them. If what we choose to do during this season fits these outer visible categories, I suspect it will raise the quality of our Advent life.

But what of an inner perspective? Let me close with the West African legend about the Sky Maiden shared by Rabbi Harold Kushner in the introduction to his book, *Who Needs God*.

It happened that the people of the tribe noticed that their cows were giving less milk than they used to, and they couldn't understand why. So a young man volunteered to stay up all night to see what might be happening.

As he waited, he saw something extraordinary. A young woman of astonishing beauty rode a moonbeam down from heaven to earth, carrying a large pail. She milked the cows, filled her pail, and mounting the moonbeam, returned to the sky.

So the young man set a trap near the cows, and the next night when the maiden came, he caught her. "Who are you?" he demanded.

She explained that she was a Sky Maiden, a member of a tribe that lived in the sky and had no food of their own. It was her job to come to earth at night and find food.

She pleaded with him to let her out of the net, and she would do anything he asked. The man said he would release her only if she agreed to marry him.

"I will marry you," she said, "but first you must let me go home for three days to prepare myself. Then I will return and be your wife."

He agreed.

Three days later, she returned, carrying a large box. "I will be your wife, and make you very happy," she said, "but you must promise me never to look inside this box."

For several weeks they were happy. Then one day, while his wife was out, the man was overcome with curiosity, and opened the box. There was nothing in it. When the maiden came home, she noticed her husband looking strangely at her, and she said, "You opened the box, didn't you?"

The man was angry at being caught. "What's so terrible about my peeking into an empty box?" he said.

"I will not be able to live with you anymore," she said. "I'm not leaving you because you opened the box. I thought you probably would. I'm leaving you because you said it was empty. It wasn't empty. It was full of sky. It contained the light and the air and the smells of my home in the sky. When I went home for the last time, I filled that box with everything that was most precious to me to remind me of where I came from. How can I be your wife if what is most precious to me is emptiness to you?"

I want this fable to remind you that you have control over your own inner Advent perspective. No one can take from you what you know is there, even if they can't see it. If your Advent box contains hopes and anticipation; if it is full of the sights, smells, and sounds of a living faith; if it contains the treasure of God's good tidings to all people; if it reminds you of the things you hope for in your better moments, then don't let anyone or anything tell you your box is empty.

There are those who look at Advent and say, "There's nothing in it." But if you have some hope, some confidence, even some suspicion that there is light in the world that no darkness can overcome, then that is more than nothing. If you have some experience of knowing that to walk in God's promised light is to lift life into new dimensions of meaning and joy, even though you sometimes stumble, sometimes can't find the light, and sometimes ignore it, then that is more than nothing. Any experience of God's light in Christ, any hope for it, is a treasure, something that no one can take from you even if they can't see it.

I wish for us all a blessed Advent, full of the treasures of God's promises. A season not only on the up, but on the up-and-up, as high and joyful as any of us hope it might be.

21

The Wondrous Gift Is Given
Mal. 3:1-4; Luke 1:39-55

More than a hundred years ago, Louis Redner, the organist of Philadelphia's Holy Trinity Episcopal Church, and the rector of the church, the great preacher Phillips Brooks, combined their talents to create a magnificent Christmas carol. The words are simple and lyric, the music a combination of flowing melody with a harmonic structure more complex and rich than most hymns.

"O Little Town of Bethlehem" came from the heart of Brooks as he recalled his visit to the Holy Land in Christmas of 1865. Like Christmas itself, the words are simple in their beauty and rich and deep in their meaning. The verses of the hymn will be an outline for our thoughts. But first the texts for the day.

Malachi 3:1-4 is perhaps the most quoted passage from this last book in the Old Testament. Anyone who has appreciated Handel's *Messiah* will find many of these phrases familiar and lovely. One can hardly read or hear them without hearing the music that Handel composed.

"See, I am sending my messenger to prepare the way before me," the chapter begins, "and the Lord whom you seek will suddenly come to his temple. The messenger of the covenant in whom you delight—indeed, he is coming, says the Lord of hosts. But who can endure the day of his coming, and who can stand when he appears?"

Malachi is Hebrew for "my messenger," and this messenger is foretelling the coming of the real messenger. The text is in the middle of seven disputes, and in this context, the messenger is speaking to those who have wearied of God. They do not disbelieve, but they have become hardened, calloused. God doesn't really matter any more.

In her 1986 book *The Minor Prophets*, Old Testament scholar Elizabeth Achtemeier gets us to the heart of the message:

> To people who think that the covenant relationship and its God are non-existent, or merely memories from the past, the Lord of the covenant will himself come. That is a frightening prospect for any age that thinks God to be absent from the world.

A wondrous gift is to be given. A messenger will come, even the Lord of the covenant himself, to refine and purify the faithful and judge the unfaithful.

The New Testament words of the Annunciation are a prophecy, much in the style of the Old Testament. One is to be born who will be named Jesus, and he will save his people. In the birth of Mary's child, a wondrous gift is to be given to the world, a gift that fits the promises spoken to Abraham and to all his posterity. Salvation, the promise of new life, is to be fulfilled in the giving of this wondrous gift who will be both messenger and message.

Now, let's return to "O little town of Bethlehem, how still we see thee lie!" To whom does the gift come? God comes to the small and insignificant. Everyone thought the King would be born in Jerusalem, the seat of authority and power. But God chose little Bethlehem, a small, obscure village six miles from Jerusalem, out in the hills of Judea.

We are very conscious of size. When photographers took pictures of Prince Charles and Princess Diana, they tried to shield the fact that he was shorter than she by having him stand on one or two steps so that he would appear to be tall and dominant. He was, after all, heir to the throne. He should not appear small by comparison to the princess.

In 1713, some men in England decided to accentuate their size by forming a club for those under five feet tall. They advertised in *The Guardian*, a London newspaper. They were to have their first meeting in December, on the shortest day of the year, at a restaurant called, "The Little Piazza." The main entree was to be shrimp. They at least could smile about size.

Size is important. It's interesting how often smallness carries a pejorative implication: we "belittle" someone; we "shortchange" them; we "put them down." It was in the "little" town of Bethlehem that the wondrous gift was given, which means the gift is given to everyone: to the small, the insignificant, the belittled. No one has to buy elevator shoes or stand on a stool to be eligible for the gift. No one has to slump down or squat to be smaller. Size is not a criterion.

In the cartoon strip *Peanuts*, one Christmas Snoopy feared that his little bird friend, Woodstock, wouldn't get a visit from Santa Claus. He thought that Santa never brings presents to "tiny nondescript birds." So he refused to tell Woodstock about the jolly old man from the North Pole. Snoopy said, "It's kind of sad at Christmas time to be a nobody bird."

There are no nobody birds at Christmas. The wondrous gift is given to small and tall, to weak and powerful, to common and exceptional people.

We're ready for verse two of the song: "For Christ was born of Mary." How does God come? In a natural way. There is no cosmic birth in some far-off galaxy like Superman. This is not a full grown miraculous appearance out of the mystery of obscurity. God comes of woman, in the simple miracle of birth, with the child kicking to be free of the womb, the push-down pains of labor, the frantic cry for air in lungs that are just beginning to function, and the necessity of diapers and swaddling clothes.

One of the classic cartoons of all times is H. T. Webster's famous 1909 drawing that celebrated the hundredth anniversary of Abraham Lincoln's birth. The picture shows two Kentucky frontiersmen pausing to visit on a snow-covered trail. Bare trees are gaunt against a leaden sky.

One frontiersman asks the other, "Any news down to the village, Ezry?" His friend answers, "Well, Squire McClean's gone t' Washington t' see Madison swore in. Oh, and Ol' Spellman tells me this Bonapart fella has captured most o'Spain. What's new out here, neighbor?"

"Nuthin' a'tall, nuthin' a'tall, 'cept for a new baby down t' Tom Lincoln's. Nuthin' ever happens out here."

Something did happen in Bethlehem. Christ was born of Mary, and in that truth, Emmanuel, God with us. God one of us, God who knows physical growing, God who knows temptation, God who knows hunger and pain, God who knows rejection, God who feels lonely, God who weeps, God who laughs with children, God who truly understands us and identifies with us, that God is born. Born of Mary, this wondrous gift not only comes to us, but is with us in natural human form.

On to verse three: "How silently, how silently, the wondrous gift is given." God comes in the silence. It is not in the noise of metropolitan Jerusalem, not in the ancient celebrations in the temple, not in the parties held by the gathering taxpayers, not even in the eating and drinking which took place at the "no vacancy" inn. The wondrous gift was given in the silence of a stable, away from the noises of the world.

Thomas Carlyle once said, "Silence is the element in which great things fashion themselves together that in length they may emerge, full formed and majestic, into the daylight of life." Silence—time to contemplate, to think and listen to the meaning of Christmas, is an important part of the gift. John Bannister Tabb once wrote a verse called "A Christmas Cradle." It goes like this:

> Let my heart the cradle be
> of thy bleak nativity
> Tossed by wintry tempests wild
> if it rock thee, Holy Child,
> Then as grows the outer din
> greater peace shall reign within.

How silently, how silently the wondrous gift is given. In silence, "God imparts to human hearts, the blessings of his heaven."

And the last verse: "Cast out our sin and enter in, be born in us today. . . . O come to us, abide with us, our Lord Emmanuel!" The wondrous gift is the gift of salvation. There is purpose in the promise. There are at least two important images associated with salvation: one is freedom from sin and wrongdoing, and the other is an abiding presence that continues to live with us.

We know the truth of having to make room in the inn. In the classic *A Christmas Carol* by Charles Dickens, Scrooge's miserliness and selfishness have to be cast out before Tiny Tim can be freed to walk again, and before old Scrooge himself can truly be alive.

All our feelings of inferiority or superiority, our personality maladjustments, our depressions, and our flabby morality have to be cast aside in favor of the wholeness and completeness offered in this wondrous gift.

Have you noticed that there is a kind of mixed emotional and spiritual reality about Christmas? We're eager for the promise and the joy to become real. Although the gift is certainly given in love, there's almost a hesitancy to accept the gift at face value.

Could it be that Malachi's message is also appropriate for us? Could it be that Elizabeth Achtemeier is right—that we don't really care that much anymore and we are ashamed of that feeling? Or could it be that, based on the way we live our lives, we aren't sure we deserve the gift?

David Mosser, minister of the First United Methodist Church in Georgetown, Texas, tells a story that may help us recognize the mixed feelings we have about this wondrous gift. Let me quote him in first person (from *Biblical Preaching Journal*, Fall 1991, p. 41).

> As a child of nine, I had illusions of being a professional football player. This made me like every other child on my street. I had an old football helmet, but I wanted a new one—a special one! Everyday I would beg my parents for it, but they said I'd have to wait and see what Santa would bring. They got quite a kick teasing me, for they knew something I didn't. They had already gotten me a Riddell football helmet, exactly like the one quarterback Johnny Unitas wore—my hero.
>
> One day in November after the typical "we'll just have to wait and see" mother's response, I proceeded to the front porch. In a rage I threw my old helmet down, cracking it fatally. I wailed out of shame and guilt and grief. I had destroyed my favorite possession. Afraid of what my father would say about my deportment, I hid the helmet and lied, saying I lost it. Later, on Christmas morning, when I received the joyous gift, my folks couldn't understand my perturbed countenance. The gift was the worst indictment of how undeserving I was. The memory is still painful.

For all of us who have angrily or impatiently failed to appreciate something valuable that we had, the receiving of a new gift somehow turns out to be both judgment and joy. We accept it with mixed feelings.

But the gift given at Christmas, more than anything else,

is a gift of love. In that truth we know that we can all "abide the day of his coming." The message is the same as the messenger. The gift turns out to be not only one who casts out, but one who enters in and makes us new: one who abides with us as Emmanuel, God with us.

This is the season of the wondrous gift, a season to remember how it was and welcome how it can be. The gift came and still comes to the small and the large, to humans as a human. It comes in the hushed expectancy of silence, to all who desire to be changed and made whole.

Receive the gift! Receive it in joy!

22

Eyes that Have Seen
Luke 2:22-40

What is it about eating buffet style that has made it so popular in the last few years? I suspect it's because the menu isn't limited. Even as you eat, the possibilities are still spread out before you. You can build your own salad, you can choose your own entree, and more than either of those, you can eat what you want and go back for more if you choose. The only disadvantage is, nobody serves you. You have to do your own work.

Let's imagine that this chapter is an Epiphany buffet, rather than an entree that is served to you. You are going to have spread out before you the kind of biblical study that goes into making a sermon. You get to choose your own ingredients, make your own applications, and build your own message out of the ingredients you choose.

Verses 22-24 of Luke 2 introduce the passage. They explain how Mary and Joseph brought Jesus to the temple, and how their trip there was to fulfill certain requirements of the law. These verses were intended to indicate that Mary and Joseph were devout parents and that they were doing everything that their faith required of them in raising their son.

When the first child comes into a family, it is not unusual for the parents to feel not only overjoyed but somewhat overwhelmed by the responsibility. Often they are moved to more elaborate care and concern for their first child than for later children. And it is not unusual that parents, thankful for the miracle and joy of birth, are more responsive to their faith when a child is born than at more everyday happy occasions.

But these verses do not suggest that the parents behaved differently because the child was their firstborn. The verses intend to convey that Mary and Joseph were devout persons, doing everything their faith expected of them in the raising of their son.

That's the first item on the buffet. Responsible faithful parenting.

Mary and Joseph and Jesus are the main characters in this story. But in verses 25-38, you will notice two additional persons. One is familiar, the other less known.

The familiar character is an old man, blessed by the Spirit of God, who is waiting "for the consolation of Israel." The Scripture indicates that Simeon was specially endowed by God. He had been promised that he would not die before he had seen the Lord's Messiah. Simeon came regularly to the temple, patiently watching and waiting.

There is another person who was in the temple everyday. Her name was Anna, and Luke described her as a prophet. Luke did not define what the term means here, though he mentioned in Acts 21:9 that Philip had four unmarried daughters who prophesied.

Anna is described as a devout woman who practically lived in the temple night and day, praying and fasting. She lived seven years with her husband after their marriage, and has been a widow from that time to her present age of eighty-four. She too appeared on the scene at exactly the right time and recognized Jesus.

Let's take the two persons in turn. When Simeon recognized Jesus he did two things. He delivered what scholars call a canticle and an oracle, that is, an announcement and a prophesy. In church liturgy, the announcement is called the *Nunc Dimittis*, Latin for "now depart." Simeon spoke of himself as a watchful servant released from his vigil. Having seen Jesus and recognized that he is the promised bearer of messianic peace, salvation, and light, Simeon knew that he was now free to die. It was not that he longed to die. Rather, God's promise to him was fulfilled. Simeon's trust in God was vindicated, and he was ready to go at God's bidding.

The announcement was more than was immediately apparent. You may recall that the announcement to the shepherds at the time of Jesus' birth—"peace among those whom he favors"—implied that Jesus came for the welfare of Israel. But Simeon enlarged the scope of the salvation brought by this Messiah. He made it clear that deliverance was in full view of all the nations and was a revelation to the heathen as well as glory to Israel. This good news was for all, not just for God's chosen people.

The oracle, the prophecy, was less joyful. In fact, it was downright ominous. Simeon said that this child would be spoken against. He told Mary that the child would be a sword that would pierce her heart. And he said that many in Israel would fall and rise because of him.

Do not take the sequence, fall and rise, lightly. New Testament scholar Joseph Fitzmeyer suggested that this already implies the scandal of the cross and the victory of the resurrection. Rejection and victory are in the prophesy, and despite the foreboding tone, there is already a suggestion that the pattern of death and resurrection will be available to many.

Anna is less known than Simeon. In fact, she is often ignored when the Scripture is read.

Anna's name has the same root as Hannah, the mother of Samuel. Its meaning in Hebrew is related to grace and favor. While Anna uttered no pronouncements and no prophesies, her role in the story was a significant one. Her devout faithfulness certainly matched Simeon's. And the spirit must have led her to the same place and time as it led Simeon.

Simeon said, "My eyes have seen your salvation." He felt his work was completed and he could be released from his watchman duties.

Anna's work was, in one way, just beginning. When she saw salvation, it was her responsibility to spread the word to all who were hoping and waiting for the redemption of Jerusalem. She became a messenger—a herald.

Now we've looked at the items on this buffet separately, let's look at them together for a moment. Here are two people, patiently and faithfully waiting for God's decisive action on behalf of the covenant people.

Waiting is not always exciting. Sometimes it can be downright dull. Even eager waiting can be exasperating. It's hard for children as they wait for Christmas morning. How many parents are asked: "Can't I open one present? Just one present, ple-e-ease." It's not easy for either children or adults to wait for something they deeply want.

But Simeon and Anna waited faithfully and in good spirit. The Greek word *prosdexomai* includes the idea of welcoming with joy what is awaited. Charles Wolfe suggests that even in the dull routine of watching and waiting, Simeon looked forward to the great days ahead rather than lamenting the passing of the good old days.

At the end of December and the beginning of January, there are always many reviews and predictions. What's your judgment about what this year's commentators said? Were their comments largely pessimistic or basically optimistic? There was some of both, but probably the pessimistic predictions caught our deepest attention.

Some people look to the new year with fear and foreboding, while others do so with hope and expectancy. Simeon and Anna must have been persons who had an expectant spirit.

Patient and hopeful fulfilling of responsibility—that's another nourishing entree on our buffet.

But there is something else represented by these two persons that I've never heard discussed in relation to this Scripture. Fitzmeyer suggests that there is a link between Luke's portrayal of Simeon and Anna and passages in Isaiah about the heralds of the coming Messiah. The heralds in Isaiah are both masculine and feminine. In Isaiah 40:9 the herald is feminine: "Get you up to a high mountain, O Zion, herald of good tidings. . . ." In Isaiah 52:7 the herald is masculine. "How beautiful upon the mountains are the feet of the messenger who announces peace. . . ."

I am pleased when congregations in my denomination, the Church of the Brethren, are willing to call both men or women to minister among them. While the Church of the Brethren has ordained women for many years now, there are still many congregations that are unwilling to recognize the right and the ability of women to serve as pastors. And there are many more that say it is right for both genders to serve but who are unable to support it in practice. Some say that they base their objections on Scripture. But here is a Scripture that scholars say links the duties of heralding to both men and women. And the word *herald* is often translated elsewhere in the Bible as proclaimer or preacher.

About half of the graduate students enrolled in Brethren seminaries are women, so we may as well deal with the issue forthrightly. I expect women pastors to be commonplace soon. Our eyes will behold it! Those congregations that refuse to give equal opportunity to women pastors will find themselves limited in leadership possibilities. And ultimately, there will be some men who will refuse to negotiate with a congregation that refuses to look at a candidate because of gender. All of this has very little to do with feminism as such; it has a great deal to do with our understanding of men and women being created in the image of God and therefore equally eligible to be servants of God in the ministry.

I rejoice in those churches that are open to considering a pastor on the basis of gifts and abilities, rather than gender. And I rejoice in the fact that we can now begin to say to the young women in our church, "Full-time ministry service is a vocational option for you."

Established patterns do not change easily, but this one will change. It will change because it ought to change, and because it is essentially biblical. It is not accidental that Luke patterns the recognition of Jesus and the spreading of the word about Jesus after the male/female heralds mentioned by the prophet Isaiah. This new reign which fulfills the covenant includes equal opportunity for all of God's children to be heralds of the good news.

As you can see, this biblical buffet offers quite a spread. There are a lot of entrees laid out for your consideration. There are a devout father and mother, a baby recognized as God's deliverance, an old man who recognizes and announces Jesus as God's light to the world and who foretells the scandal of the cross and the wonder of the resurrection. Also, there is an old woman who recognizes and then assumes the responsibility to tell the good news to everyone.

All together, this passage provides a model of faithful fulfillment of responsibility and a model of who God's heralds are supposed to be. There is plenty here for any of us to think about and finish our own sermon.

Allow me one more specific application. Do you share my concern that so many of the moral and ethical values upon which a good society is based seem to be eroding? Honesty, trust, compassion, decency, respect; we can go on down the list. Do you realize that almost any value or standard that we would classify as important is supported by the teachings of Jesus?

If you agree, then it is high time that our children and grandchildren begin to understand why it is that we believe what we believe and do what we do. We do not make choices just because it is the right thing. The right thing is supported by tenets of the Christian faith, which we heard and learned from those who loved and cared for us. Our eyes had the chance to see, to comprehend, to absorb. It is a legacy I'm afraid too many of us forget to pass along.

One year the newspaper for the area in which we lived chose to change its daily format on the day before Christmas. The whole front page was good news, with a little footnote that normal front page items could be found on page three.

This biblical buffet which is background for celebrating Epiphany is front page good news. Simeon makes clear that it is not just for the special people, but for everyone.

But Anna completes the table of entrees. Not only are salvation and light for everyone, but anyone who has eyes to see may become a herald. In fact, Anna represents the rest of us more than Simeon. When our eyes finally see, it is not time to quit, to relax as if our watching and waiting is over. It is not a time to celebrate that our work is done. It's time to go out and tell anyone who will listen that we have eyes that have seen the good news.

Enjoy your buffet.

23

Understanding the Son's Death

Rom. 5:1-11; Luke 15:1-10

Let me tell you about a woman named Virginia. I have not seen her for years, but when I knew her, she was a brilliant young mother, full of energy. She was outspoken and had just been elected mayor of her suburban community.

Virginia was not the kind of parishioner who could be called passive or docile. She never swallowed anything I said without carefully inspecting it.

I liked her. I liked her honesty, her intellectual struggle. Such people keep a pastor honest. I never knew what she would say to me at the door, but I remember clearly one Sunday during Lent.

"Earle, I don't like Lent," she said.

"Do you want to say why, or shall we talk later?" I asked.

She went right on. "Lent accuses me of being responsible for Christ's death, but for the life of me, I don't know what I had to do with an of it."

I waited.

"If Christ died for me, then why? What did I do that caused it? You spoke of ransom and atonement as if there was some kind of infraction, some kind of law broken, as if I personally did something for which Jesus had to pay to bail me out."

I was secretly impressed that she was understanding what I had said. But she punctured my balloon.

"I don't like that kind of view of God," she said. "If God is love and God is like Jesus, then why is God so angry that Jesus has to die to make things right between us and God?"

Away she went. And suddenly I didn't feel as good about what I had said.

I doubt if Virginia's feeling is unusual. I think there are many of us who have trouble putting together theological words and statements about the "necessary" death of Jesus and our understanding of the teachings of Jesus about God. So this sermon is a part of my continuing struggle to understand the Son's death.

While we will focus mostly on Romans 5, we'll start with Luke 15:1-10. Notice the context of these parables. The scribes and Pharisees are grumbling because Jesus is associating with tax collectors and sinners. It was a radical change to have a Rabbi show consideration to such people.

Jesus tells them a story which says there is more joy in heaven over one lost sheep found than over ninety-nine already saved. Not good news for the insider—the Pharisees were not happy campers over this announcement. Jesus was telling them that he was sent for everyone, not just Israel. Such inclusiveness was a new and unsettling idea.

What Jesus was really asking them to do was to change their concept of God. Most of us do this reluctantly, if at all. It may be that before we are finished with Romans 5, you may feel that I am suggesting that you change some of your concepts of God.

While working on this sermon, I picked up a book titled *A Stone for A Pillow* by Madeleine L'Engle. She asked some of the same questions Virginia asked, only in a different way.

Reading Nicholas Berdyaev's *Revelation and Truth*, L'Engle came across his assertion that a grave problem in the

Western world today is that we have taken a "forensic" view of God.

Forensic means having to do with crime. Forensic medicine helps the coroner determine if crime caused a death. Was the death accidental, self-inflicted, or homicide?

In our judicial system an accused person is presumed innocent until proven guilty. A forensic doctrine of God, however, assumes that we are guilty until a way is found to placate the divine anger: some way to purchase or receive an acquittal that makes us acceptable to God.

Let me share a paragraph from *Homiletics* (vol. 2, no. 1, p. 44), which describes it this way:

> There is going to be a trial. And you and I will be judged by the Lord God almighty. And we will be okayed in that trial. We will be justified forensically, made right in that trial. Not by lawyers, not by briefs filed in our behalf. But by a person. "Father," Jesus will say, "He has sinned, but sought repentance. She has tried to turn from her evil way to serve you. Therefore on my behalf, for my sake, forgive him and her." And the Father has promised he will.

That little paragraph is a fairly succinct summary of a traditional view of the necessity of the son's death. But if that is the only way to understand the son's death, then we must ask Virginia's question in the most pointed and direct way we can: Did Jesus have to come and get crucified, because only if he died in agony on the cross could this bad-tempered father forgive his other children?

It may be time for us to look carefully at our understanding of God. For God is not less than Jesus, and nothing in the words of Jesus about who his Father is and who he himself is would point to that kind of view as justification for his death. That most known Scripture verse says, "For God so loved the world that he gave his only Son"; it does not say that God was so angry that the only way to settle the score was to have his son killed. You see, we may need to change some of our thinking about the Son's death.

The words we use don't help us any. They almost imply a forensic understanding. Take the word *ransom*. That's a central concept in traditional crucifixion theology. It means to cover or pay the cost for the recovery of something. It is a word used fourteen times in the Old Testament and four times in the New Testament.

Or take *propitiation*, used in the King James Version, or *expiation*, used in the Revised Standard Version. These refer to something which appeases or makes amends. Or consider the word *atonement*. It is used eighty-seven times in the RSV Old Testament, but not even once in the New Testament. In the New Testament, the word is translated as reconciliation. The root meaning of the word is not paying some price to make up for mistakes or errors; it means what it says: to make one—at-one-ment. It means bringing together.

Now alongside some of those traditional understandings of the Son's death, let's consider the words of Romans 5. Listen to the language. "We have peace with God through our Lord Jesus Christ, through whom we have obtained access to this grace in which we stand . . . For while we were still weak, at the right time Christ died for the ungodly."

It is clear from this language that Christ died for us. It is clear that we are separated from God. It is not clear that the Son's death was a sacrifice that paid any dues, ransom, or fines that were required by a God who assumed us guilty until our innocence was bought. There is no mention of appeasing an angry God; there is strong language about a way provided for us to be in relationship with God.

The word *access* is important. That has to do with a way from one place to another. Jesus spoke of himself as *The Way*. He spoke of himself as one with the Father: "if you know me you have known the Father." He spoke of himself going to the Father and our following him. He spoke of his death being necessary because of our being lost.

Madeleine L'Engle once said that sin is discourtesy—discourtesy pushed to its extreme. It is simply not caring. It is lack of at-one-ment. It is lack of relationship. It is choosing to be separate when we were made for relationship with God.

In the language of Jesus, it is being lost. Therefore, being saved is being found. There is no hint of the forensic in this scheme. There are no images of crime that must somehow be justified by the sacrifice of a life.

I'm coming more and more to wonder if Berdyaev isn't on to something when he said that belief in hell is a lack of faith. It is to ascribe to Satan more power than to God, or if that is not true, then it is to ascribe Satanic forensic characteristics to God.

To be separated when one longs to be together is hell. To choose to be separated when someone longs for relationship is hell. To be separated from God is hell. To live in an unforgiving lifestyle is hell. To require vengeance to rectify wrong as a means to justice is hell. Most of the hell we experience that is not natural calamity or the finite frailty of our humanness, is the result of choosing to turn away from God, not the sentence of an angry God who sends us to a place of punishment for disobedience.

When you think of it, isn't it true that the entire Bible focuses on God's effort to find some way for humankind to choose the wonderful relationship that is waiting for us in the mercy and love of God? Sin is not the little or big crimes we choose to commit. These occur because we are out of relationship with God.

The sin the Bible says we need help with is separation from God. And God loved us enough to send a Son who helps us to understand God and see the way into the relationship that is intended for us.

It hardly seems accidental to me that the story of the prodigal son immediately follows the parables of the lost sheep and the lost coin. They are part of the same theme—lost and found, separation and reunion. In the relationship between the prodigal and his father, there is joy and welcome—not a single word about paying up before you get back in. It is assumed that if you want into the relationship, you are already unhappy with the separation. The choice to be there is all it takes.

No, Virginia, there is no ransom, no atonement in terms of paying a fine, no cruel death as a sacrifice to appease a forensic God. But, yes Virginia, there is a loving act in the giving of a Son, which leads to a cruel death because humankind chooses not to receive him and be in the relationship with the kind of God we really have. And in that act we recognize at-onement.

Every year we hear of the tremendous inheritances that have never been claimed by the rightful beneficiaries, treasures that they are not aware of, treasures that they don't even know how to be aware of. The Son's death was not payment of a life to appease a forensic God. The giving of the Son was an act of self-giving on the part of God that ended in suffering and continues to end in suffering so long as we refuse to be in relationship to God.

It was and is crucial to God that we not be lost, that we have a clear way to be found. The Son's death made permanent our access to the God who loves us and who eagerly and patiently waits for us with open arms. It is an inheritance of joy that the Son still offers us if we will choose it.

24

Easter Is Coming, But Not Until. . . .

Ps. 116:1-9; John 11:1-45

Imagine you've decided to treat yourself to an evening at a good restaurant. You even eat a light lunch to enjoy dinner more. When you arrive, which would you rather have the hostess place in front of you as she seats you: a three page menu, simple in explanation, and divided clearly into categories that you understand, or an eight-page, foreign language volume that requires ten minutes to read before you have enough information to make an intelligent choice?

To be sure, there are times and places that are suited for a long and leisurely experience of choosing what to eat. Indeed, for some, the choosing is part of relishing the whole event. For others, the choosing is like shopping, an exercise in fear that if I choose one thing, I may miss something I would like much better.

I prefer the condensed style of menu to the massive, historical novel approach. Like the little boy who wrote a one sentence book report—"There is more in this book about penguins than I cared to know"—I pick up a large menu, and say to myself, "This tells me more than I care to know about the food served in this restaurant."

Some of you may have experienced that kind of feeling in the scriptural menu for this morning. The full story of

Lazarus may be more than you cared to deal with on this particular Sunday morning. There are all kinds of appetizers and a la carte issues to catch our attention. More than that, the main entree is difficult enough in itself to digest, even when we've chosen it.

Don't you wonder why Jesus, who was only two miles away from Bethany when the word came of Lazarus's illness, stayed two days longer in the place where he was? In the 911 climate we live in, we'd surely expect better than that. Isn't it interesting that when he finally decides to go, the disciples feared for his safety? Doesn't it make sense that when Jesus said, "Lazarus has fallen asleep, but I am going there to awaken him," that the disciples would say, "if he has fallen asleep he will be all right?" Isn't that just like them to misinterpret what's happening.

What of Thomas the twin? We could think long on his statement to his fellow disciples: "Let us also go, that we may die with him." What of the reversal of roles that transpires with Mary and Martha. It is Martha who went out to meet Jesus, almost bitterly hurling her hurt at him: "Lord, if you had been here, my brother would not have died. But even now I know that God will give you whatever you ask of him."

This is the woman who, on a different occasion, was worried about whether the meal was ready to be served and the fact that she had to take care of it all by herself. Where did she get this kind of insight, this kind of understanding of the power of Jesus? Mary was the one who sat at Jesus' feet, listening and comprehending. And when Jesus said, "Your brother will rise again," Martha the busybody housekeeper made a profound statement: "I know that he will rise again in the resurrection on the last day."

When Jesus says, "I am the resurrection and the life," Martha makes an even more astounding statement: "Yes,

Lord, I believe that you are the Messiah." Her faith pilgrimage is enticing. We could easily spend time on that issue.

This story also includes that favorite verse of all young boys who need to recite a memory verse and want to get it over with as soon as possible—the shortest verse in the Bible: "Jesus wept." We might take the time to ask why. If Jesus knew that he was going to raise Lazarus from the dead, why would he weep? The onlookers said, "See how he loved him!" And some of them said, "Could not he who opened the eyes of the blind man have kept this man from dying?"

And, if we are paying attention, we might notice how important it is to the story that it be very clear that Lazarus was really dead. He was in the tomb four days, one day longer than legally necessary to make sure a person was dead. If the count of days was not enough, the smell itself left no doubt.

So much here to choose from. As one person said, there is so much here, that a pastor would do better to choose one of the other lectionary options for the day.

Indeed, this passage may offer more than we wanted to know. We might understand the story to be a simple proclamation—a message that Jesus raised Lazarus from the dead for the express purpose of showing that he had power over death. That meaning is certainly here.

Martha understood that we will all be raised in the end. But many people didn't know that, believe it, accept it. It's almost as if Jesus was saying: "This one time, I will give all the doubters a sign. I will show that I have power over death. Easter is coming for all who believe." That is wonderful news in itself. Few of us would want to be without it.

But what about those of us who belong to the company of inquiring minds that want to know? Is there something else beside the sure knowledge that the resurrection is coming? Even Martha was not satisfied. "Lord," she seemed to be saying, "I know that we will be raised in the end—but the end is a long time away. What about now? If you had been here, my brother would not have died."

Those standing around echoed the sentiment. Perhaps they echo our own contemporary question: Couldn't this man who opened the eyes of the blind have kept his friend from dying?

And the answer is no. We're at the main menu item here. Jesus could not keep Lazarus from dying. Jesus has power over death, but not power to keep it from happening. It is our created nature to die. None of us will escape that. And the tears Jesus sheds are for the pain, frustration, anger, grief, loss, and emptiness that so many of God's children feel in the presence of death.

Far too often death comes before we are ready for it. It comes at the wrong time, before we've finished what we would like to have done. We call out, in the same spirit as Martha, "Why can't you keep us from this?"

Once in a great while, we are ready for death. Once in a while we are able to say, as I was able to say recently for my father, "it is a blessing." We say that because there is a sense in which age and infirmity create situations where some loved ones are dead while they are legally alive. And we say that because some of us, who are responsible for infirm and extremely incapacitated older loved ones, aren't sure how we can continue to responsibly care for them.

But even then, even when death is a blessing because the quality of life is so poor, we must still deal with the ultimate truth of death. We must deal with the sense of loss, the end of a generation. Sometimes we must deal with pangs of guilt over the relief we feel when a person is released from a less than acceptable existence.

The story says Jesus wept. I think he wept because death for a person created to live is always some form of pain or loss. It is always an ending to what was begun.

We cannot be spared from this. The cherished and important promise of life after death cannot keep us from the reality of dying. Jesus can raise Lazarus from the dead, but he cannot keep him from dying. Easter is coming—but not until we die.

Actually, that is not the whole truth. We are blessed with preliminary understandings of what Easter is like. Do you remember when five skiers were missing after an avalanche in Colorado? Did you see the unrestrained joy when the brother of one of the skiers rushed into the arms of the one who was saved? A miracle! New life for those who, while they struggled to hold hope high, had already begun to grieve.

We are blessed with preliminary understandings of Easter; little resurrection appetizers which are a precursor to the main event. I know it personally.

A man rolls down the corridor of a hospital toward the operating room, aware that in an hour, a surgeon will saw open his chest, and have his heart lying out on his ribs, working to sew in patches of veins so that blocked arteries can function again. He rolls along the corridor, at peace with God, but knowing full well that the operation may or may not work. When he opens his eyes after the surgery, drugged and in pain, he nonetheless knows what resurrection is about.

A woman goes through the dark valley of chemotherapy, dying a little each time the chemical invades her. But after the treatments are finished and she understands that they have succeeded, she knows what resurrection is.

In a TV series from a few years back, a character who accidentally contracted AIDS is walking with a friend along the sea. He says, "You can't almost die and come back the same." He had experienced a kind of resurrection. He had been returned to the joy and pain of living.

Have you noticed how people talk after they have faced their own mortality? Almost all of them say something like, "I'm going to focus my life on those things which are really important."

Anyone who has experienced forgiveness has some foreknowledge of what resurrection is about. In the May 1992 issue of *Circuit Rider,* Jaime Potter-Miller shared a touching story:

> My son Jordon came running to me, tears pouring from his big blue eyes. The cry was one of pain and frustration as he toddled to me holding up a pudgy arm. Jordan was eleven months old. He had six teeth, four on top and two on the bottom. On his arm was a vicious bite, already turning purple, with a full set of teeth marks. Our three year old daughter Janna was found and reprimanded in my characteristic manner. When I wanted to make sure she paid attention, I'd cradle her cheeks in my hands, grasp her ear lobes between my thumb and forefinger, and speak slowly, "Now watch my mouth, Janna, this is important!" She was solemnly but lightly spanked with instructions to never, ever, again bite her poor baby brother, and she was denied Sesame Street privileges for the rest of the day.
>
> That evening, as I was helping her get ready for bed, and lifted her into the tub, I noticed an ugly bruise on her little bottom Surrounding the center of the bruise were six, distinct teeth marks, four above and two below. . . . I said, "Janna, honey, how did you get that bruise?" She looked at me matter of factly and said, "That's were Jordon bit me before I bit him."
>
> "Why didn't you tell me?" I asked. And she said, "You didn't ask me, mommy."
>
> I told her I had been an unfair mommy and that she could spank me if she wanted to. But she reached over, took my face in her little wet hands and said, "Watch my mouth, Mommy, this is important. It's okay."

Anyone who lives through a time of genuine confession has experienced a kind of resurrection. True confession always includes the kind of living death that comes when you recognize that you've really done something wrong, and in the recognition of that wrong, plead for and receive forgiveness. A person who has experienced forgiveness knows something about resurrection, about new life given to take the place of the old.

There are two ways to get ready for resurrection. One is to recognize it when it happens, while we are still living; the second is to understand that it can't happen in the final form Jesus promised unless we live through death.

The Lazarus story is not a resurrection story like Easter. It is a story of new life, accomplished in such a way that the promise of eternal life is carried in a convincing and once-for-all-time manner. It is a story that says, Easter is coming, but not until we have lived through Lent, not until the pain of being human is faced in the experience of death.

In raising Lazarus, Jesus showed he has power over death. But in the story, Jesus is also helping us understand that he does not have power to keep us from dying.

Jesus wept because he understood our human resentment, our pain and sorrow about having to die. Easter is coming—but not until we die. Meanwhile we always have the possibility of new life while we are alive, the possibility of spiritual and physical renewal to remind us that resurrection is something real that we can hold onto right on into eternity.

25

A Day of Gladness
Ps. 118:14-28

In his engaging book, *Travels With Charley*, John Steinbeck says that

> Some days are born ugly. No one knows what causes this, but on such a day people resist getting out of bed and set their heels against the day. When they are finally forced out by hunger or job, they find the day is just as lousy as they knew it would be. On such a day it is impossible to make a good cup of coffee, shoestrings break, cups leap from the shelf by themselves and shatter on the floor, children who are ordinarily honest tell lies; this is the day the cat chooses to have kittens and housebroken dogs wet on the parlor rug.

When we have the kind of day Steinbeck is describing, we say, "It's one of those days."

But the writer of Psalm 118, the Old Testament text chosen for Easter, seems to be having a good day. "I thank you," he says, "that you have answered me and have become my salvation. The stone that the builders rejected has become the chief cornerstone. This is the Lord's doing; it is marvelous in our eyes. This is the day that the Lord has made; let us rejoice and be glad in it."

For the psalmist, there was joy because the Lord had made "this day," whatever day it was, a special day of victory, celebration, and gladness.

Easter is a day whose message contributes to the unique character of the Christian Faith. Easter is, in itself, the cornerstone in our faith. It is fundamental to our belief. It is a day of gladness, a day which the Lord has made and in which we rejoice.

Why is this a day of gladness? Have you seen the TV commercial that shows a beautiful child's face and eyes as an announcer says, "Would you trust those eyes to just anyone?" Then we see the child being fitted with glasses so that she can see what she couldn't see before.

Easter is that kind of day of gladness. It fits us with glasses of faith that allow us to see what we would not otherwise be able to see.

On a clear day, a popular song once said, you can see forever. That's one reason Easter is a day of gladness: no haze, no fog, no overcast. No smog. No blurred vision. No astigmatism. Death is swallowed up in victory.

There is another reason, and we can find it in the story of Simon Pereins, told by Guillermo Ochoa, a newspaper feature writer in Mexico City. Simon was arrested by the Inquisition back in the seventeenth century and thrown into a dungeon cell. It's hard to imagine how we would feel, especially since being arrested was the same as being found guilty. No one was ever released. It was the end of life. The very best anyone could do was linger on in a cell that was dark, damp, filthy, and full of rodents and bugs. That was your whole life until you died.

But Simon Pereins found something to do. He took clay from the floor of the cell, added some of his meager food, and mixed paint. Then he took fragments of cloth, string, and straw from his clothes and blanket and made them into a paintbrush. He used his cell door as a canvas, and on that door he painted a picture of the Virgin Mary and the Child Jesus. He painted the picture in 1667, a picture that was so beautiful that his inquisitors were convinced that he had seen a heavenly vision, and they set him free. The painting still exists, it is called the *Altar Del Perdon*, the altar of pardon.

Easter is a day of gladness because the risen spirit of the living Christ is made available to us in any situation or circumstance in which we find ourselves. Easter can make any day a good day. In whatever contemporary dungeon of despair we may be, Easter allows us to take the simple necessities of life and mix from them a paint with which to show the glory of our faith. Easter allows us to face any day and every day with some sense of gladness.

One of the chewing gum manufacturers used to have a clever ad. The company set its catchy phrase in the context of some historical fact, such as Magellan being the first man to sail around the world. A sailor calls out, "How long shall we continue to sail in this direction, Captain Magellan?" And Magellan answers, "I'm not talking while the flavor lasts."

The good news of Easter lasts and lasts. The Lord has favored us with the saving news of Christ's resurrection, and we can't stop our gladness while the flavor lasts.

We are celebrating a day of gladness: a day that can make any day a good day, a day which lasts and lasts, and a day from which we can see forever. This is a day that the Lord has made; let us rejoice and be glad in it.

A Prayer

What a day of gladness, O Lord. On this day we remember some of the best news the world ever received. In the familiarity of the ancient story of the resurrection, we find hope. In the good news of Easter there is fortification for beliefs and feelings that become shaky without reinforcement. It is good to rehearse the Easter message again.

But for some of us, O God, the joy is not as deep, not as invigorating, not as secure as we wish. O God, can the worn-out news be revived? Are there not ways our spirits can soak up the reality of resurrection and be free to genuinely rejoice? Call to mind for each of us the times we have had a second chance. For some of us, a second chance at life, a second chance at love, or a second chance to mend brokenness, or repair a mistake. Were we not resurrected?

Call to mind for each of us the changes in life. Those of us who are teenagers are no longer five or six. Those of us who are thirty-something are no longer teenagers. And those of us who are senior citizens are no longer thirty-something. We do not have the same worries we used to have; none of us are limited by the same understandings. We have been through mental and physical resurrections that help us to realize we are different persons than we used to be.

O God, help us to see the cycle of life itself as a parable of death and resurrection. When new things are possible here, we find it easier to believe new things are possible in the life to come. Sometimes the condition of life controls the joy of special days. We pray for all who are bowed down by bad news; for all who have lost loved ones; for all who face uncertainty. Strengthen them and give them hope.

We are in that time of year when we expect the hibernation of winter be replaced by the reality of spring. Life will blossom all around us. And we will rejoice in it. But let new life also blossom within us. For that's what Christ gave us on this day.

In his name we pray, Amen.

26

He Is Risen
Matt. 28:1-10

I'm glad you are here today. I'm glad, because I have good news for you: Christ is risen!

For many of us, it may be hard to get excited about this familiar message. I remember some years ago a grocery chain that advertised on TV and said, "Nothing new—just the same old story—everyday low prices."

From all the response I saw on your faces, I might have said, "It's Sunday, the temperature is fifty-five degrees with an expected high of sixty-four."

To put it another way, it's highly possible that I would have gotten more response from you if I had announced that, as a reward for your presence this Easter morning, the church board had voted to give each family fifty dollars, and you could collect as you leave church.

While Easter is a time of joy, there is, nonetheless, a certain sameness about its annual appearing. It is, after all, the same old message. There is no way I can give you something brand new, something astonishing right off the celestial press this morning. There is only this ancient message: "He has been raised from the dead, and . . . you shall see him."

Whether that message is received joyfully and celebrated as good news depends upon how we perceive it. Is Easter mostly a special worldwide holy day, or is it an experience? Is it a doctrine or is it a lifestyle? Are these words of yesteryear meant only to inspire faith, or are they special greetings for today?

Let's agree that Easter is history. It is an event that happened. I read once of a man accused of stealing. As he stood before the judge, the judge said, "At least four people will testify that they saw you take this article from the store."

"Sure," the man replied, "but I can bring you forty people who will swear that they didn't see me take it."

When talking about the historic truth of Easter, negative testimony has no weight as evidence. Skeptics may argue; thousands may say it's a myth; form critics may debate the fallibility of the gospel writers. When you shake it all down, we are obliged to take at face value the testimony of the witnesses who were involved, not those who were absent.

Still, even if we successfully argued the historical truth of Easter it would not make it all we want. Even if you believe, as the famous Harvard law professor Simon Greenleaf did, that the resurrection holds up under all kinds of application of the rules of evidence, there is still a sense in which accepting it is a matter of faith. Somehow, Easter as history does not fulfill our eagerness for good news. We want more than good news yesterday. We want more than "He Arose."

Let's agree that Easter is also future—that it is good news for tomorrow. In a world that is so conscious about the future, so filled with insurance, retirement benefits, social security, and investments, the good news that the future is secure beyond the time when all monetary preparations lose their effectiveness should be cause for joy. The promise of life after death makes social security look like peanuts.

Skeptics find all kinds of questions to raise about how we can know the future is secure. They see a vast difference between the facts related to social security and the facts related to eternal life. The denominational tradition I grew up in— the Church of the Brethren—has many unique characters in its history. One of them was a man by the name of Reuel B. Pritchett. In his book *On the Ground Floor of Heaven,* written with Dale Aukerman, Pritchett says,

> What will it be like, strolling the halls of eternity? . . . Suppose I would say to an old green tobacco worm, treacherous looking little critter: "Tomorrow you'll spin a cocoon with a thousand silk threads, and in a few weeks you'll cut out with beautiful downy wings, float in the wind overhead of everything, and sup the nectar from ten thousand flowers, whereas now you're squirting this old green tobacco juice."
>
> Suppose I take an egg that's just beginning to pip. I hold it to my ear and listen to the life in it and say to that egg, "Tomorrow, little chick, you'll crack the dome of this home of yours, crawl out under the vast dome of heaven with your mates and see God's sunshine." The chick can hardly have any inkling of what's about to be.
>
> Or the little chimley swift, born and bred down in the flue of a dark chimley. Suppose I'd say to the frail creature, "Tomorrow you'll rise up out of this old sooty narrow place. You'll spread your wings and skim wide and far under the radiant blue of heaven." He wouldn't understand. Down in there he can see only a sliver of sky.
>
> I'm the worm, the egg, the chimley swift. We all are. Jesus tries to tell us what we're to be. We can't understand. Marvelous beyond belief has it been to grace God's earth, this waiting room to eternity. What will it be like to grace the strands and slopes of heaven?

Skeptics abound, but many of us hold this Easter promise about the future, in faith, and it is strength to us. We believe that Christ goes before us and waits on the other side of this life to welcome us.

Still, we want something more out of Easter than yesterday and tomorrow. We want Easter to have something for today. Somewhere in our expectations, most of us would like some experience of the risen Lord in this life, some good news for now.

Easter is the news of death and resurrection. Something is discarded, something received. Old life is given up and new life is taken on; one form replaces another.

In his letter to the Colossians, Paul used language that spoke of putting off the old life and putting on the new. That means change. Reuel Pritchett's word to the old green tobacco worm might have been, "You can become something new, but that cocoon has got to go." Easter is only average news for all of us who want a change, but do not want to change. We want things to be different without letting go of the restrictive cocoons that comfort us, protect us, and feed our needs.

It's a strange thing, but when, as a hospital patient you leave intensive care, it is supposed to be a sign of improvement, a sign of change for the better. But in the middle of that there is often a little sense of the loss of security, a loss of special attention, a loss of round the clock monitoring and immediate care. Often there is some fear of how it's going to go. Change, even for the better, is not always attractive to us in its first stages.

Easter calls us to say yes to resurrection as a way of taking on new life. When we refuse to change, we say no to resurrection. We do so—

- anytime we live primarily out of anger, peevishness, and disappointment or cherish the right to feel sorry for ourselves;
- anytime hostile feelings toward another are the dominant emotions that affect our decisions;
- anytime we choose loneliness or brokenness over the responsibility of relationships;
- anytime we make the gospel of Jesus Christ a sweaty drudgery rather than a joyful freedom.

We say yes to resurrection—

- anytime we give up the cocoon of peevishness over how life has treated us and begin to choose those things which make for growth and joy;
- anytime we lay to rest an old hate and replace it with acceptance;
- anytime we take on the work of repairing a love relationship;
- anytime we rise to a new day with thanksgiving and eagerness;
- anytime the preciousness of life is far more clear than irritableness over what it's withholding from us.

A parent says yes to resurrection in telling a troubled teenager, "I love you, I care about you, but I can't control your life or be responsible for what you do anymore."

A teenager says yes to resurrection anytime he or she can say to troubled parents, "I love you, I respect your wisdom. I cannot be all you are or want me to be, but I will be the best that I can be."

Death and resurrection, putting off the old and putting on the new, giving up the old and receiving the new—that is one way the living Lord greets us in our today.

I began by telling you this good news, "He is risen." Let me share with you a true story about how another group of people received this very same announcement. It was told by Nicholas Goncharoff, a former Soviet Army tank officer.

On Easter Sunday, in a day when communism was still in power in Russia, he was in one of the country's larger cities. All of the churches had been closed except one, a large Orthodox Church. It was the only house of worship for over 300,000 people.

The church was soon crowded with Easter worshipers, so those not able to fit indoors stood outside. In the street, however, the Communist Party had organized a demonstration. Firecrackers exploded, and a band played loudly to disrupt the service.

The next day, the Party ordered the population to come to the city square. Special speakers lectured for four hours, suggesting that religion was the opiate of the people and that it was for the uneducated, for weaklings.

When they were done, the chairman asked the crowd, "Are there any questions?"

No answer.

"Do you have any comments?"

No answer.

Then a small thin man said, "I would like to say three words."

The small man came to the platform and turned and faced the thousands of quiet people. Then he leaned toward the microphone and said distinctly, "Christ is risen."

I wish our reaction would match the reaction of those standing in that square in Russia. The announcement was not received as old stuff. As those simple words came over the speaker, the thousands roared a mighty response: "He is risen indeed! He is risen indeed!"

The police emptied the square; the little man was spirited away. But the people had had their Easter. Not just an Easter of yesterday, or tomorrow, but an Easter for today.

I'm glad you're here today. I have good news for you: Christ is risen! He is risen indeed!

27

Spirit Plus One and More
Acts 2:1-13; 9:1-19

A Sunday school teacher had cleverly taught her class to recite the Apostles' Creed by giving each child one phrase to learn and repeat. At the class presentation, the students did beautifully.

"I believe in God the Father Almighty, maker of heaven and earth," said the first child. "I believe in Jesus Christ, his only Son, our Lord," said the next. And so on they went in turn until they came to the child who said, "He ascended into heaven and sitteth on the right hand of God the Father Almighty, from thence he shall come to judge the quick and the dead." At that point an embarrassed silence fell until a little girl spoke up and said, "Uh, the little boy who believes in the Holy Ghost is absent today."

It's Pentecost Sunday. I hope we won't hit an embarrassing silence because people who believe in the Holy Spirit aren't here today. No, I won't ask for a show of hands.

We all know that the Holy Spirit is not front-page news. Sitting around talking about the Holy Spirit is not normal conversational fare for most of us. There isn't even a line in the Conventional Wisdom section of *Newsweek* on the subject. But once a year, at least, on Pentecost, we take time to think about the Spirit and its work.

Maybe belief is not the main issue anyway. One wonders if those who first experienced the Spirit believed in it before it happened. That lovable, gravel-voiced trumpeter, Louis Armstrong, is supposed to have said that rhythm is "what, if you've got it, you don't need a definition, and if you don't got it, no definition is any good anyway."

So, on this Pentecost Sunday, we won't try to define the Spirit. It isn't necessary, and in fact may not be helpful. Instead, we'll focus on the possibility of being open to the Spirit and what we might expect to happen if the Spirit were to take hold of us.

At the turn of each decade, *The Christian Century* publishes a series of articles by current theologians on "How My Mind Has Changed." In the April 23, 1980, issue, German scholar Jürgen Moltmann made these pertinent remarks:

> Christianity is now challenged by a revitalization of religion. Those critics of the church who had reckoned with a 'death of religion' (Marx and Lenin) miscalculated. Those who had hoped for a 'religionless' Christianity (Bonhoeffer) were disappointed. Those who proclaimed "God is Dead" have now learned to fear the God of the Ayatollah.

"But," he goes on,

> the new search for religious experience is deeply ambiguous. Today the challenge of religion meets . . . and pulls us in two opposite directions at the same time. We hear it in the call for security, authority, and belonging. But we hear it also in the cry for freedom, spontaneity, and community. On the one hand, the Christian church moves toward the bureaucracy of an organized religion; on the other, it moves toward the spirit of voluntary community.

That's a long quote, but it seems to me to be a perceptive analysis for our time. We do live in a day of religious hunger. The fast pace, mobility, and rootlessness of our society are taking their toll. In response, people are becoming more aware of the deep religious hungers that are inherent within us.

Moltmann is right. There is a hunger both for a secure foundation upon which to build the house of our faith and for a freedom of spirit that will not be controlled by institutions or bureaucracy.

Is it not strange to you that anxiety and uncertainty should be the controlling mood for those of us who live in what is viewed by the rest of the world as a rich and safe nation? Perhaps you remember Abraham Maslow's theory. He said that only when the basic needs of a society were met could the society then move along his famous steps to fulfillment and self actualization. But that has not happened. Would you classify the progressive West as being more contented and happy than the third world East? We have less economic upheaval, but are we any happier? Meeting basic needs does not seem to be enough to set us on the road to higher things.

The 1960s and 1970s saw political and social upheaval. But the answers were not in the violence, nor in the possibility of social salvation, nor in withdrawing from the middle class. Now we have come partly through the yuppie age, and whether we are new graduates, baby boomers, or old timers who have lived through several economic cycles, the scent of rampant materialism is strong in our nostrils and the hunger for something different still plagues us. That nagging hunger for a religious experience, something to give ourselves to that which puts meaning and significance to our very lives, will not be quelled. Perhaps Berdyaev is right: "Human beings are incurably religious."

Kermon Thomasson once wrote an editorial in the Church of the Brethren publication, *Messenger,* about a barn spider that dropped down out of the dark corner of the loft to make a new home on the floor. The spider built a new web that proved effective and lasted well. One day she examined the long taut line of silk that led back up to the darkness of the loft. Deciding that it was no longer needed, the spider snipped it. And the web collapsed.

Our hunger, our openness to the religious, is partly nurtured by the fear that we may have, by intent or neglect, snipped the line that holds the web of life together. The revival of interest in religious experience has its roots in the longing for significant meaning and purpose in life. And the point I'm making is, that longing, that hunger, is creating more openness to the Spirit right now than we have known for some time.

More openness? Yes! But let us also recognize that there is some real hesitancy amid any eagerness we admit to. Let's face it—the spirit stands for change, and something in us does not like to change. If we had to choose, we would like our most secure and untroubled days baptized as the norm. We want to be supported, affirmed, secure; we do not want the hazard of change.

You may recall Robert Louis Stevenson's story of *Dr. Jekyll and Mr. Hyde.* By experiments in his laboratory, Dr. Jekyll produced a secret elixir which, when consumed, freed him of all inhibitions, and allowed all the aggressive, hedonistic, uncontrollable emotions of his personality to take over his life in the form of Mr. Hyde. The story both fascinates and terrifies. Once in a while the fantasy of freedom from all inhibitions is fun to play with in the mind. Yet I doubt that our desire for freedom would lead any of us to actually down a draft of Dr. Jekyll's elixir.

But let your mind play with the idea a little more. Reverse the story. Suppose in front of you were little glasses filled with an elixir of the Holy Spirit. Would you be any more eager to gulp down a brew filled with the Spirit, if you knew that drinking it would bring out all the best in you, if you knew that you would then make decisions that were only in keeping with the spirit and teaching of the New Testament? Would you drink it if you knew that all decision would be made in honesty, in justice, and with true concern for the well-being of others? Would you drink it if it changed you into what you think a true Christian ought to be?

Even though we are in the midst of a revival of religious concern which creates a new openness to the Spirit, we, like others in our societ, have mixed feelings about the prospect of basic change. It's very possible that we would like change only on our terms—enough but not too much. For many of us, being a new creature through the baptism of the Holy Spirit may be a fascinating fantasy but a fearful reality.

So what can we expect if the Spirit happens to come upon us? The confusion and mystery of Pentecost may not be as helpful to us as the story of Paul. Damascus bound, Saul was on a mission of religious indignation against Christians who are upsetting the spiritual equilibrium of his people. But he himself was upset by the Spirit, knocked down by it. The Spirit knocked a new sense of mission into his head and heart, and in so doing, knocked a hole in his reputation as one of the rising young stars "in the organization."

The dynamics behind the experience aren't clear. Maybe Paul's association with those he was persecuting created some sense of hunger to have in his life what he saw in theirs. Maybe he was open to something new. In any event, he received it. He didn't fight it.

If his experience has some normative quality in it, let's recognize that an experience of the Spirit is not a lonely experience. Such a conversion must surely occur in the privacy of the human heart and soul, but it is not a process that can be completed and confirmed alone. There needs to be the Spirit, plus one and more. Ananias was the plus one in Paul's experience, and the community of faith was the more.

Paul was blinded by the experience; immobilized by the confrontation. Maybe he wanted to stay in the euphoria of the experience. Maybe he didn't want it tarnished by the reality of life. Maybe he wanted the joy without the change. Maybe he didn't want what the Spirit required. Whatever the reason, he was immobilized and needed help to get from the experience itself to the living of it in his life. He needed someone to relieve the scales of ecstasy, to help him see what the coming of the Spirit really meant in his life. And a messenger of God, a brother in the faith, Ananias, came and ministered to his blindness.

There is a suggestion here that, in a true religious experience, the Spirit does not zap a person while others simply stand around and marvel. The Spirit is confirmed, identified, and tested in relationship with others. New life needs more than the spirit; it needs the plus one and more of others to help interpret and provide ways for the Spirit to be expressed.

There may be those who insist the Christian faith is best practiced in personal privacy. Mystics and ascetics over the centuries have espoused this solitary approach. But the New Testament is clear: there is no such thing as an isolated Christian. It takes the Spirit plus one and more to knock the scales from our eyes and help us see our new life and mission.

Baptism of the spirit is not freedom from community. It is baptism into the need for community. We cannot change in aloneness, because we do not live in aloneness. The community is the body in which the Spirit works. We are all the one and more who encourage, temper, and test the presence of the Spirit.

It is clear that the Spirit brought genuine change to Paul. It took away his old purpose, his old job, his old success, and left him with a new life and mission. Would we risk drinking that little cup of spiritual elixir; would we pray for the gift of the Spirit? Only if we were open to it and also open to the genuine change it would bring.

Perhaps the change is not as painful as we think. We always think of becoming a new person as giving up cherished things. Maybe it's not that way.

In his commentary *Epistle to the Romans,* Donald Grey Barnhouse described how he outgrew the desire to play marbles:

> I never had to come to the place where I said, "Oh I am a big boy now, and big boys shouldn't play marbles. So I will make a great effort live without playing marbles." It happened a different way. One day I was playing marbles with a group of small boys and some older boys came by. They looked at me and said, "Hey, kid, can you field a ball?" "Sure I can," I replied with more vigor than accuracy. "Well," they said, "we're short a fielder. Get out there and see what you can do."

Barnhouse says he went out and was ready to play his head off to keep up with the older fellows. "When the game was over, we older boys, as I then classed myself, walked down the street past the little fellows who were playing marbles, I did not go back to marbles. I had graduated. I did not give up marbles, marbles gave me up" (p. 18-19).

Something in us wants to move on to something better. That part of us resists mediocrity, does not cherish a half-lived life. Something in us is attracted to genuine meaning and vitality; a sense of purpose, and an assurance that our lives will amount to something.

Something in us is willing to move from marbles to baseball, from shallow games to life commitment. That hunger and openness make us candidates for the coming of the Spirit and the change that comes with it. It welcomes the Spirit as it moves not alone but always plus one and more.

28

Division In the House
Luke 12:49-56

Have you ever had someone tell you something, and when they finished, you wished they hadn't told you? It happened to me one morning in late September, around 1975.

The phone rang in my little space in the Church of the Brethren General Offices in Elgin, Illinois. A woman with a nice voice asked if it was me. I said "Yes."

"Is Jon sick?" she asked. Jon is our youngest son.

"No, at least he wasn't when he left the house this morning," I responded.

"Well," she said, "I think you should know that, counting today, he has missed four days of school in a row."

I was stunned. "There must be some mistake," I said.

"No mistake on our part," she replied. "This is his fourth day of absence."

I mumbled something about appreciating her call and said I would look into it.

"I certainly hope you do," she responded.

I thanked her again and hung up. I would have just as soon she had never told me. On the other hand, it was crucial that I know.

We eventually got the situation straightened out. Jon had indeed been skipping school. He knew that the school system allowed students up to a week's absence during the school year without penalty to grades. Without consulting his parents, he had decided to take all his days for the whole school year during one week in September.

The feeling I had when the lady from the school told me that piece of unwelcome news is similar to the feeling I had when I discovered that the text for this morning was Luke 12:49-56. I would have just as soon not known that.

I have never before preached on this text. Even when it came up in the lectionary rotation, I chose one of the other options. I was on the verge of doing this again when the thought flashed through my mind, "maybe I should look into it." And it seemed almost as if some word from the Spirit said, "I certainly hope you do."

In these verses from Luke, Jesus speaks of fire and division. One person has said that this is surely one of the most difficult passages in the gospels. Another person, in the process of discussing the text in a group setting, said bluntly, "Jesus had a bad day!"

At first glance, it seems that way. We picture Jesus as a strong but gentle man. He is firm yet patient, encouraging rather than judgmental, thought provoking, but not caustic. Yet here he is, speaking in a manner most troublesome to us: "I came to bring fire to the earth, and how I wish it were already kindled!" Then he continues, "Do you suppose that I came to bring peace to the earth?"

"Of course," we answer. "We hear that at Christmas and many times during the church year. You are the Prince of Peace. Sometimes in church, we bless each other by spreading the peace of Christ."

But he interrupts us. He has not come to bring peace at all: "No, I tell you, but rather division!"

I would rather not have heard that.

As members of the body of Christ, we place a high priority on family life. We expect the church to be a place where values that strengthen family are articulated and encouraged.

Yet Jesus says, "From now on, five in one households will be divided, three against two, and two against three . . . father against son and son against father, mother against daughter and daughter against mother, mother-in-law against her daughter-in-law and daughter-in-law against her mother-in-law."

I think these are all things we would have just as soon not have known. Here we are, hoping for some kind and encouraging word, and Jesus is talking about divisions in our house and what it takes to follow him.

Is Jesus having a bad day? One commentator speaks about the passage this way:

> One immediately senses the passion and drama. The first person language, the anguished wish that the fire were already kindled, the admission of distress, the questions posed in such a way every single reader wants a yes . . . only to find it a no, the vivid description of the divided families. . . . It all adds up to an ominous scene, pictured in evocative terms. Appropriately, the translators punctuate each sentence with an exclamation point. (*Texts for Preaching, A Lectionary Commentary,* Westminster John Knox Press, Year C, p. 476ff.)

Is Jesus having a bad day? He is on the road to Jerusalem. Just before these sayings, he has warned his disciples against hypocrisy. He has told them the parable of the rich fool, who thought that life consists in the abundance of possessions. He has admonished them not to worry about what they will eat, drink, or wear and has warned that a person cannot serve two masters. There are cautions to be watchful and prepared.

Then we find these troublesome, angry sounding words. What are the fire and the baptism he speaks of? In the Gospel of Luke, fire occurs repeatedly as a symbol of judgment, a time of reckoning. The reference to baptism is best understood as Jesus' impending death.

It is almost as if the trauma of what is about to happen wells up within him. He sees his own fiery time and wishes it were already over. He sees the day as a time of crisis, demanding repentance and changed lives, and is saddened that those around him who can read the signs of impending rain or the onset of hot winds from the desert cannot, or will not, take the time to read the signs of the time. Indeed, he probably is having a bad day.

But is that all that this passage shows? Or is there a side of Jesus' ministry and message that we conveniently skip over most of the time? Surely, the blessing of being a disciple is more to our liking than the cost, and there are undercurrents in his words that have to do with cost. Surely, the benefits of grace are more attractive than the pain of disagreement, dissension, and rejection. Yet there are undercurrents in his words that remind us of those kinds of brokenness. I have the sense that, even though we might rather not think about it, there is something here we really ought to look into.

There is a hint early in the life of Jesus that seems rather benign at the time but which suggests the trend toward division in the house. Early in the Gospel of Luke, when Jesus' parents presented him in the temple, Old Simeon rejoiced that he has lived to see the salvation which God intended for all people. Then he said to Mary: "This child is destined for the falling and the rising of many in Israel, and to be a sign that will be opposed so that the inner thoughts of many will be revealed—and a sword will pierce your own soul too."

Later, when Jesus was twelve years old, his family made their yearly trek to the temple. On the way home, Jesus disappeared. When his parents missed him, they frantically returned to Jerusalem.

It took three days to find him! He was in the temple, sitting among the teachers, listening and asking questions.

Irate, Mary confronted him: "Child, why have you treated us like this? Look, your father and I have been searching for you in great anxiety."

"Why were you searching for me?" Jesus responded. "Did you not know that I must be in my Father's house?"

But Mary and Joseph "did not understand what he said." A division in the house, already, at age twelve!

We know little about the time between that event and Jesus' appearance at the Jordan to be baptized by John. Luke 2:52 says simply, "Jesus increased in wisdom and in years, and in divine and human favor."

There is much we would like to know. What kind of teenager was Jesus? What kind of family life did he have? If he had brothers and sisters, what were his sibling relationships like? Did he ever fuss because more was expected of him than the younger children? Would he have experienced anything like imaginary lines in the back seat of the car which no brother or sister dared even violate, not even the air space immediately above it?

Did Jesus and his father have special quality times together as they worked together in carpentry? Did Joseph secretly hope that Jesus would take over the family business? Were Joseph and Mary hoping against hope that their firstborn would be able to do his God-appointed work by living a fairly normal life? Would they see grandchildren in their old age? Would the community favor they felt in their eldest son hold up during his prophesied ministry? Oh, how they must have hoped against hope that they would be able to hold their head high among their neighbors.

The questions pile up for us. And we wonder, why this tirade against the family?

But there aren't many answers. All the family history, the childhood anecdotes are hidden from us. According to the *Interpreter's Dictionary of the Bible* (p. 876), the ancient world had no interest in what you and I would call personality: those combinations of physical, mental, emotional, and spiritual characteristics that arouse our interest and make us curious about how or why persons turn out to be the person they are. There is no trace of this interest in the Bible or in any other ancient Semitic literature. Neither the Greeks or Romans even had a word for *personality.* So early family life, the formative periods of growth and family relationships were not discussed. Apparently, however, there were not enough divisions to interfere with the fact that Jesus was the kind of young person who fostered human and divine favor.

Why do we ask such questions? Perhaps because there are experiences in life that remind us of the truth of Jesus' words. Don't we know about divided houses: three against two, two against three, father against son, daughter alienated, in-laws at odds? Even in the best of times we experience divisions in the house. And we want to know whether Jesus lived through those things also.

Is that what he was warning us about? We might be able to accept the tirade against the family if he meant the normal kind of rebellion and reunion, rejection, reconciliation, and sibling rivalry that are part of almost every family.

But I don't believe we can get off that easy. Jesus does not say, "You will experience division, two against three." He says, "I came to bring fire. . . . Do you think that I have come to bring peace. . . ? No, I tell you, but rather division."

Recognition and acceptance of normal family problems may be understood as something in keeping with the spirit and teaching of the New Testament, but that understanding will not suffice as an interpretation of this text. We must dig deeper.

Let me introduce you to a family. They are a husband, wife, daughter, and son. You are meeting the family in the late 1960s, when the daughter is well married, the son is single. The father is a successful businessman, though he came through hard times when his family was young. During those lean years, the church was a source of strength and encouragement to him. The exercise of his faith within a faith community was dear to him. His family and ours were friends, and he was present at my ordination as a supporting deacon.

On a summer vacation at my home, I ran into him downtown, and we talked for a few minutes. I asked him how his family was.

"Earle," he said, "we're all well, except I'm having real problems with my son. He's finished college, you know. But I don't understand him. He tells me my faith is old fashioned, he wants faith to have meaning in the contemporary situation. It does for me, but not for him. He tells me the hymns we sing don't have any meaning to him, and they are dear to me. He tells me the language of the church no longer speaks to him, and I love the familiar, the old hymns and the way things have been, and don't want too much change. He wants to go into Brethren Volunteer Service, I want him to start earning a living.

"He tells me money isn't important," my friend went on, "and that the Christian faith teaches us so. He tells me he isn't interested in the family business, that the Christian faith calls him to a life which needs to be spent in some kind of work which will benefit humanity.

"I tell him I've given my life to benefitting those who seek my services. I tell him it's not riches, but what we do with what we have that counts. On and on it goes.

"I thought the family that prayed together and went to church together, stayed together. It isn't working that way. His faith and mine are very different. What can I do?"

You'll not be surprised that at the ripe old age of thirty something I didn't have an answer for him. Nor would I have an easy, one-sentence jewel to drop in his ear today, thirty-five years later. But notice, this is not normal father/son division. There is an ingredient here that is more painful to the father: there is a division in the house over faith in and faithfulness to Christ. The father and son disagree strongly over how to be faithful in continuing the work of Jesus.

You heard the father's words: "I thought the family that prayed and went to church together, stayed together." We're on to something, I think. It may well be that Jesus does bring division in the family to the very heart of what differing members feel they are called to do to fulfill their discipleship.

A few years ago a man said to me, "If my daughter asked me if I would support her decision to go into the ministry, I would say, "No way." But suppose the daughter felt a calling to be in the ministry? That would be not peace, but a division in the house. A man in a group discussion about this text told his fellow participants that he is still out of favor with his parents for having chosen to devote his life to the ministry. It is true, isn't it, that the choice to follow Jesus may indeed bring divisions in the family?

This is true not only in the immediate family but also in the family of the church, in the corporate body of Christ. Thanks to good historical help from Don Durnbaugh, let's go back to a Church of the Brethren Annual Conference in Louisville, Kentucky in 1969, when a paper on "Obedience to God and Civil Disobedience" was being discussed.

Conference attendees felt fraternity and unity were absent in the speeches they heard. Imagine the anger, hostility, and judgmental speeches from older members of the church when young men who were refusing to register for military service, were burning their draft cards or were fleeing to Canada asked for official support for their position.

Historically, the denomination had recognized conscientious objection to military service as an appropriate stance.

Under that position, the objector would still register, make an important witness, then seek an alternative way to serve the country. That position was controversial enough in its own right, causing many a division in homes throughout our brotherhood during and following World War II.

But these young men in 1969 firmly believed that registration in itself constituted support of the war. And to all the speeches which sought to put them down, to call them revolutionaries, to remind them that such approval could be interpreted as supporting rioting, to all speeches which reminded them that civil disobedience was supposed to be a last resort only after all legal means to correct injustice had been tried, to all voices that pleaded with their "misguided understanding of what it was historically to be Brethren" they simply kept saying, "these are things you taught us in Sunday school. . . . Our stance is consistent with what we have learned in church about discipleship and commitment to Christ."

There was a huge division in the house during this conference discussion. Had the issue been put to a plurality of Church of the Brethren members across the denomination, it would have suffered a resounding defeat. But the amazing thing was that the delegates voted by a two-to-one margin to support those who were practicing civil disobedience. Though the vote was questioned the following year by many who felt it did not adequately represent the denomination's stance, it withstood the test. It is as if deep in our own corporate consciousness, we understood that we must find some way to support those who, in the way they choose to be faithful to Christ, are radically different than most of us.

Faithfulness to Christ can cause divisions in our houses. In *Pulpit Resource* (vol. 23, no. 3, 1995, p. 32), William Willimon reminds us that

The true conflict in our attempts to follow Jesus, is not conflict between what we love and what we ought to hate, but rather the conflict between our loves. We love our family, would do most anything for them, and yet Jesus is also demanding our love. . . . Most of the really wonderful things that happen to us in life happen in the family. Most of the really terrible things that happen to us in life happen in the family.

When you think about it, our experience of family at the personal and corporate level really does encompass the brightest and darkest moments of our life. Willimon helps us further.

I don't really know whether or not Jesus' words (in this text) are an attack upon our family life. . . . I do know that today's gospel is a strong, public declaration, in words fierce and fiery, that following Jesus is no tame, domesticated peaceful affair. When two conflicting values collide, such as discipleship to Jesus and loyalty to the family, there will be divisions in the house.

Perhaps we need to rest our questions in that kind of observation. But let's try to put Jesus' saying in words as if he were speaking to us in our own time. It might go something like this: Do you think that following me will bring only peace and joy. No, I tell you, it will also bring division in your houses and homes. When families of five work out their faithfulness, there will likely be three against two; there may well be father against son, and daughter against mother, and in-laws alienated. When you get the weather report on TV, and you see a low and high pressure system colliding, you say there may be a severe storm, and it happens. If you see a stalled high pressure system and it is hot and humid today, you say it will continue tomorrow and it does. How sad. You read the signs of earth and sky, why are you unwilling to read and understand and accept the cost of discipleship?

I don't believe Jesus was just having a bad day. I think he was having an honest day. Nothing he says here denies that the good news is full of promises about peace, joy, fulfillment, and contentment in close family relationships and rewarding relationships with him and God. I think he was reminding us that in the best and worst of times, following him has its difficulties, even as faithfulness to God was causing him pain and suffering, including separation from his family. I think Jesus was reminding us that there will be demands on life and times that will make persons who are near and dear to us unhappy, and that this will be painful.

Such a message is something we might rather not have heard. But it is surely something we need to look into and be reminded of.

29

The Seeds of Peace

James 3:16-4:6; Mal. 2:4-9

A while ago (Sept. 23, 1985) a community college teacher by the name of Jaime O'Neill wrote a "My Turn" column in *Newsweek* titled, "No Allusions in the Classroom." He began with a quote from Josh Billings suggesting that it is "better not to know so much than to know so many things that ain't so." Then he went on to talk about the game that goes on when a teacher tries to find out what the student doesn't know, and students try to hide their ignorance in every way they can.

O'Neill decided to give his English composition students an eighty-six question, general knowledge test. There were twenty-six people in the class ranging from ages eighteen to fifty-four. Here's a sample of some of the things they knew that aren't so. Ralph Nader is a baseball player. Charles Darwin invented gravity. Christ was born in the sixteenth century. "The Great Gatsby was a magician in the 1930s; Franz Joseph Haydn was a songwriter in the same decade. Sid Caesar was an early Roman emperor, Mark Twain invented the cotton gin, and Socrates was a great Native American chief.

You can see why Mr. O'Neill is concerned that we know so much, but that so much of what we know ain't so.

Is it possible that O'Neill's concern in education can be transferred to those of us who relish our denomination's identification as a "peace church?" Is it possible that we have so grown up with peace that a good bit of what we know about it isn't so?

You remember that when Jesus rode into Jerusalem (*Jerusalem* means "city of peace") he wept bitter tears and said, "If you, even you, had only recognized on this day the things that make for peace." He spoke that way because Jerusalem knew so much about peace, but much of what it knew wasn't so.

In Jerusalem were a host of patriots, zealous in national pride, who spoke as if peace were the center of their purpose. Yet they spent their hours plotting and preparing for armed combat with the enemy, as if preparing for war was the way to peace.

Sound familiar? Some have estimated that the world has spent one million dollars a day on armaments since the time of Christ. Or that the billions a week our world now spends for military purposes would provide food, water, housing, health care, and education for everyone on earth for a full year.

Did you know that in 1984 the State Department won an award for creating the worst euphemism? It approved a new word for peace in its statements. Instead of *peace*, writers were instructed to use "permanent pre-hostility."

Preparations for war are still seen as the way to peace. It's amazing the number of peace church people who basically believe that. We know a great many things about peace, and much that we know isn't so.

Jesus looked at Jerusalem and wept. In Jerusalem were a variety of religious leaders, wise in the interpretation of the Scriptures, knowledgeable about the language and promises of peace. Yet they spent hour upon hour defending their positions against each other, searching for ways to put down and defeat one another. Each group was sure its way was the only way. All the while, outside the comfortable walls of the privileged religious folk, the common people cried for spiritual and physical necessities.

The church is one of the biggest property owners in our country. But we spend more time making people know our teensy weensy differences than we do in using our wealth and power in working together for the good of all of us.

More than three decades ago, Martin Luther King Jr. chastised the church for its failure to be in the forefront of the struggle for social and racial justice. Those of us who lived through that time know that the church came in for the benediction rather than the call to worship.

It is shameful, but often those of us who call ourselves pacifists are more willing to demonstrate to the world how we like a good fight among ourselves than we are eager to demonstrate peacefulness. People in the early centuries of the church said, "see how they love one another." You don't hear that much these days.

It is shameful, but often those of us who claim to be peacemakers jump into the battle against social evil and become positively militaristic in the way we witness to and promote peace. We walk on people, call them names, stereotype them, and refuse to listen, all because we believe our cause is just. We know a lot about peace, and much that we know isn't so.

Jesus looked at Jerusalem and wept. In Jerusalem were thousands of everyday people searching for relief from pain, confusion, want, oppression, and emptiness—sure that if they could have what they wanted, they would be at peace. Sound familiar?

Do you know anyone who is really at peace with what they have? I mean really willing to leave the issues of material assets and security for the future right where it is? Do you know anyone who is not worried about whether what they have now will be enough to have tomorrow? Do you know anyone who doesn't have symptoms of the sickening virus that infects us with the notion that if we only had the basic necessities of life for all the people of the world, we could all live in peace?

Yet the New Testament is clear—a person's life does not consist in the abundance of things. That is, peace is not related to abundance or lack of abundance of things. We're from a peace church. It's in our genes, and we're proud of our heritage. We know a lot about peace, and a lot of what we know isn't so.

Can we rethink some of what we know? Can we discard some of the things we know which aren't so? Here before us is this simple little verse from James 3. "A harvest of righteousness is sown in peace for those who make peace."

William Barclay said that translation is a correct and literal translation. But on the basis of other biblical study, he said the verse might also be translated to say that the seed, which one day produces the reward which righteousness brings, can only be sown when personal relationships are right and by those whose conduct produces such relationships (Barclay, *The Letters of James and Peter*, Westminster, 1958, p. 114).

Let's look a little at the biblical understanding of peace to see if he's right. The word for peace in the Old Testament is *shalom*. According to the *Interpreter's Dictionary of the Bible* (K-Q, p 705), shalom is a state of wholeness possessed by a person or groups of persons. Shalom may involve health, prosperity, security, or spiritual completeness with, no special distinction made between any of those. In fact, in the Old Testament, any distinction made between secular and religious peace is made only for analytical purposes.

Shalom is a wholeness determined and given by God. It is individual and it is communal; it is national (therefore secular) and it is religious (therefore spiritual). In the Old Testament, all peace is of God, and the one condition for peace is the presence of God. External conditions, either good or bad, ultimately have nothing to do with shalom.

In the Old Testament, peace and righteousness often go together. The effect of righteousness will be peace (Isa. 32:17), to be at peace is to be upright (Mal. 2:6), and to be at peace is to practice justice (Isa. 59:8). And since the covenant is the relationship that restores wholeness with God, the covenant and peace are inseparably joined.

In the New Testament, the word for peace is *eirene*. In classical Greek it means the absence of hostility. That meaning can still be found in Ephesians 2:14-17 in words regarding reconciliation between Jews and Gentiles, in 1 Corinthians 7:15 in words about domestic peace, and in Romans 14:19 in words about happy personal relationships.

But the New Testament meaning of eirene is broader. The word is concerned with restoring right relationships between God and persons (2 Cor. 5:19; Rom. 5:1; Col 1:20). It can even mean peace of mind, or serenity. There are some who have trouble with this meaning, as if somehow it is beneath the dignity of what the word peace really ought to mean. But it's there: in Romans 8:6, in Galatians 5:22, and in John 14:27, where the gift of peace is offered to the fearful and the afraid.

Now what's the summary of our mini-Bible study? What may we designate as the seeds of peace if we take the biblical understanding of what peace is?

- Peace is a gift of God which comes in right relationships between God and persons, and between person and person, because the first is impossible without the second.
- Peace is not dependent on any other external circumstance; therefore, it cannot be commuted to us or taken from us by any external circumstance.

- Peace cannot be given by us to another; that is what we do cannot create peace for another.
- Having the gift of peace, we are required to live it and sow the seeds as peacemakers.

Let's try this biblical understanding of peace on for size. Does this concept of peace mean we should witness to our government? Of course it does. We must.

During the 1980s, according to one source, members of Congress said they had never received as much citizen contact on any issue as they did regarding provision of U.S. aid to the Nicaraguan *contras*. The Reagan Administration's request for military aid was defeated 219-211.

Those who called to oppose the aid policy planted seeds of peace at an opportune time, I believe. By refusing aid, we did not create peace for that part of Central America, but we acted peacefully in refusing to contribute to war.

We must witness to our government. I am convinced that it is absolute folly to be continually debating whether to spend billions to beef up military preparedness and do little or nothing to end the suffering present in today's world. A massive "Food for Peace" program would help the farmers of this country and help the needy around the world. We can say so, loud and clear, and tell our government we want it. But we need to recognize that a highly successful "Food for Peace" program would not give or bring peace to anyone. It will minister to need; it would be a righteous thing to do, but the external reality of less hunger will not guarantee peace.

Mark this well: We do the cause of peace no favor if we lead others to believe, or if we ourselves are seduced into believing, that if the world had what we have economically, it would be at peace. That is not true biblically, and we know it would not be true in practice because we have far more wealth than other nations in the world have, and yet we are not at peace with ourselves. It is not things we have, but being in a right relationship with God and neighbor which makes for peace. And our conduct, what we do for others, must help produce such relationships.

Does this biblical understanding of peace mean that we should speak out against violence in the media? We must. According to the National Coalition on Television Violence, 13.3 acts of violence occur in an average prime time show. Sixty-one percent of all TV viewing features themes of violence and hostility. The average child will see more than 200,000 acts of violence by age sixteen. If your child watches MTV, you can bet the visuals and lyrics constitute a constant invitation to the joys of violence and sex.

Given research which shows that there is some direct imitation and some desensitizing that happens when violence becomes a norm, we should surely work at reducing violence in the media. And we should work at limiting and screening the TV shows viewed by our families. A true peacemaker would jump at controlling something which would lead to more peace.

If you aren't sure what media violence does to an individual, try an experiment on yourself. For two days, don't read a newspaper or magazine. Don't watch any television. Use the time you would normally spend on these things in walking, reading good literature, or filling your soul with fine music or art. See what happens to you at the end of two days. My guess is you will feel more at peace.

Now take care. I am not advocating withdrawing from the world. But the excessive media diet we all consume keeps us fearful and afraid, and on the edge of hostile and aggressive feelings. We adults can keep up with the news without the volume of aggressive news to which we submit ourselves.

Should we have spoken out against apartheid in South Africa. Yes! We should have. But we needed to be very careful in taking action that forced others to what we viewed as justice. True peacemakers do not coerce another into acts of justice by acts of violence. They persuade by reason, lifestyle, or by taking upon themselves personal danger as a witness. The early Christians uprooted the injustice of the Roman Empire, not by economic boycott, but by living according to their convictions, even if it meant ending up as the entree on the menu for some lion.

If there must be sacrifice or danger to make a point, the peacemaker places jeopardy on him or herself, not on those already suffering injustice. Gandhi made his point by fasting, by threatening his own life as a way to convince his own people to repent. The command to love one's neighbor, even if that neighbor is an enemy, will not allow us to mistreat another, even if it is only economic inconvenience. Again, peace is not something we give another through social reform. We must be in a right relationship with God and neighbor so that our conduct helps to produce such a relationship.

Shall we help those who are fleeing injustice in Central America? Of course. Placing jeopardy on ourselves rather than sending them back to die is the act of a peacemaker. Shall we send persons to Central America as peace representatives? Of course. But we must be sure that their witness is a witness of love and a witness that opposes violence by whoever lives by it. We may lay our own lives on the line, but we cannot force others by our witness to do what we are not willing to do.

That great peaceful presence in the history of the Church of the Brethren, Elder John Kline, rode back and forth across Civil War battle lines. He was suspected by both sides because he gave medical attention to anyone who needed it, regardless of the color of his uniform. While Kline abhorred the evil of slavery and the evil of war, he never chose sides in the conflict, nor reduced his peacemaking to supporting the side that was the lesser of two evils. John Kline was in a right relationship with God and neighbor, and his conduct pointed to producing such relationships.

I hope you see clearly that I am not speaking against a strong concern for justice. The urgency to respond to injustice and oppression and human is need is as unrelenting as ever. But we must be careful not to confuse peacemaking with prophetic witness. We must be careful not to confuse fighting evil with doing a thing of peace. To fight evil with violence is never justified.

And we must be careful that what we say in the cause of peace is true. In many of our churches, there is a poster that says, "A modest proposal for peace: LET THE CHRISTIANS OF THE WORLD AGREE THEY WILL NOT KILL EACH OTHER." But that is far too modest. It is not even true to the New Testament, which would not allow us to kill anyone, Christian, Muslim, communist, or terrorist. On the basis of this modest proposal, it would have been possible for one of Hitler's S.S. troopers who was a member of the state church in Germany to participate in killing the Jews in good conscience. I know the poster does not intend that. But we must be careful that what we say is true.

Here are some things about peace which, on the basis of a biblical understanding of what it means, I believe are true. Peace is not so much a matter of safety as a lack of animosity. It is not so much the security of power as it is the unwillingness to be threatened by power. Peace is not just the absence of war, it is the presence of harmony within life. Peace is not just existence without hostility, it is existence with purpose and meaning. Peace is not being without anger, it is being with fairness and grace. It is not being minus an enemy, it is being plus a neighbor. Peace is not absence of disagreement, it is presence of community.

Several years ago, while recuperating from an illness, I had the opportunity to spend time with a Rubik's Cube. It did not take long to discover a truth about that frustrating piece of engineering genius. You must begin in the right way, or you will never make any headway. If you don't get the middle edge pieces to match the color of the very middle piece first, you can't create a solid color on one side. But even when you get the principle right, there's enough to do to keep you busy for a long time, longer than most people are willing to spend. We need to be willing to spend the time necessary to make any headway towad peace.

We are a peace church. We know a great deal about peace. But we must relearn the truth that the harvest of righteousness which is peace is sown in peace by those who make peace. Only conduct that produces right relationships by those who are already in a right relationship with God and neighbor can be counted as the true seeds of peace. If we don't have that right, our peacemaking isn't going to work. But even when we get that right, there's enough to do to keep us busy for a long time—maybe a whole lifetime.

30

With the Loud Cymbal

Ps. 150

This sermon is shared in oral style. The preacher I heard deliver it is unknown to me, and all efforts to recover his name have failed. He was an impressive African-American man, over six feet tall, a well-educated man, distinguished looking, with a voice like seventy-six trombones. He shared the sermon as a personal experience in wonderful black preaching style. Which means it was not just a sermon; it was an event full of drama, cadences, and literary repetition.

There are many differences between this and the original, I've tried as faithfully as memory allows to reproduce it. It's a story that ought not to be lost and a fine example of what I call "memory handles." Since hearing it, I've never attended any orchestral presentation where cymbals were visible in the percussion section without thinking of this event and the simple and profound application he made at the end. I invite you to enter his world and let him bless you as he has me.

Now, brothers and sisters, any sermon has to begin in the Word of God and end there if it's to be worth anyone's time. So I want to begin with this wonderful, powerful doxology that comes at the end of all the Psalms—the last one, the 150th Psalm.

This is not a passage of Scripture that calls for reflection and meditation. It is not a call to prayer; it is an anthem.

One does not read this *pianissimo*. You get all your wind together in your lungs, open up all the stops, and proclaim it with all the fortissimo your voice can handle. If you have your Bibles follow along.

> Praise the Lord!
> Praise God in his sanctuary;
>   praise him in his mighty firmament!
> Praise him for his mighty deeds;
>   praise him according to his surpassing greatness!
> Praise him with trumpet sound;
>   praise him with lute and harp!
> Praise him with tambourine and dance;
>   praise him with strings and pipe!
> Praise him with clanging cymbals;
>   praise him with loud clashing cymbals!
> Let everything that breathes praise the Lord.
>   Praise the Lord!

Say Amen!

Ghetto children know what noise is. It's daily fare in New York City, not at all like the quiet of this rural Illinois countryside. Ghetto children know what noise is, but they don't often have the opportunity to experience harmonic noise. One time I learned about beautiful noise.

My father and mother did not want their son to be limited by the ghetto community. They wanted something more for me than their wage and hour work. One day, when I was about six, my father said: "Son, I want you to have more opportunity than I ever had. I think you ought to take piano lessons."

Now you know, that didn't excite me on bit. But I tell you this. If your dad is six feet, four inches tall, weighs two hundred forty pounds, lays his hand on you and says, "You're going to take piano lessons," there is little doubt as to what you are going to do. And I did.

My father was no dummy. He knew the kind of piano teacher to get. She was about five feet, ten inches tall and weighed as much as my father. And when she said, "Play!" you played! And when she said, "Practice!" you practiced.

She had a little stick she used to tap out time on the edge of the piano, and every once in a while it would slip over and tap my fingers when they weren't doing what they were supposed to do. When she was displeased and frowned, it was like seeing the wrath of God on her forehead. And when she smiled, it was like God's rainbow sent to good old Noah. She was judgment and mercy, and I was afraid of her and I loved her. When she hugged me, I sort of sank into her and just disappeared until she let me loose. It was wonderful.

I was no child prodigy, but I learned. Between my dad and Mrs. Jackson, my piano teacher, I had no choice. But something seemed to be missing. So one day my dad laid a hand on my shoulder and said, "Son, I want you to have more opportunity that I ever had. I want you to get culture."

I had no idea what culture was but knew if my dad wanted me to get it, I would. I soon found out it was to come to pass through a plan cooked up by my dad and Mrs. Jackson. Getting culture meant going to hear a symphony.

I didn't know what that was, but I knew I was going, and I knew it was something like church because I had to wear my Sunday clothes. And I knew I wasn't afraid because my piano teacher, Mrs. Jackson, was taking me, and there wasn't any better protection in the whole city. So here we went, this lovely great woman in one of the world's most unique hats, and a little spit- polished six-year-old ghetto kid.

It was special all the way: first a taxi ride, then the great huge building, then the big room with all the people in it. I could look at the size of the room (probably the biggest in the world), see all the gold and velvet decorations, and try out the padded seats that went up and down all at one time.

God love her, Mrs. Jackson knew the answers to all three hundred questions I asked her in the first ten minutes.

Then I heard something! A single note—one pitch. Then there were other sounds, big and little sounds, sounds like I had never heard before. There were a lot of people, all playing something, doing their own thing with the sounds all mixed together. I thought it was some of the most beautiful noise I had ever heard. I leaned over to my teacher and said: "Psst—I like culture. I like the symphony."

"Shh!," she said, "It hasn't even started yet. They're just tuning up. Wait till you hear the real thing."

Then the real thing got ready to happen. The lights dimmed. A man walked onstage with a little stick which told me he had to be a music teacher. He tapped the stand, all the people came to attention, the instruments went up, and everyone waited. The stick came down. The sound was magnificent. It filled every little space in that great room, and it ran around all through the gold and velvet curtain, and I thought I had died and gone to heaven. I thought my little heart would burst with the beauty. It was the real thing.

I leaned over to my teacher and said: "Psst—I like culture. I like the symphony." And she smiled and patted my head, and I saw God's rainbow in her eyes.

I don't remember what symphony it was. It was long, but there was enough to watch and hear to last a long time. I tried to figure what sound came from what instrument. I watched first this player, then that one.

Then I saw him. Everyone was busy doing something except one man seated to the left. He just sat. I watched and watched and finally couldn't stand it. I leaned over to Mrs. Jackson, nudged her and said, "Psst—that man. What's he doing just sitting?"

She went "Shhh!" I saw the wrath of God on her face.

So I sat back and wondered. The longer he sat there, the

more I wondered. After what seemed a week, I leaned over and nudged Mrs. Jackson and said, "Psst! That man up there on the chair behind all that stuff, what's he—"

"Shhh!" she said. And I saw the wrath of God in her eye. Then it softened and she said, "Be patient. Just you wait. You'll see." So I waited and waited.

I watched the violin players, and then my eyes would flip over quick to the man. Nothing! Then I watched the trombone players, and I'd peep to see if he was moving when I wasn't looking. Nothing. Then hallelujah! Amen! I saw him move. He leaned over until I couldn't see him. I thought, "He's tired of waiting too. He's going to sneak out." Then he started to come up and I saw them, two great shining gold things, round like plates, one attached to each hand.

I nudged Mrs. Jackson. "What's that that man gonna do?"

"Shhh! she said. Then she leaned over. "They're cymbals and he's going to hit them together. Wait till you hear it!" And her eyes said it would be something special.

I watched him. Then he started to stand, and he lifted the cymbals up high in the front of himself. He held them and held them. And I waited and waited, and finally I couldn't stand it any longer so I stood up and shouted, "HIT 'EM!"

You know how fast a rattlesnake strikes. Mrs. Jackson was faster as she slammed me back in the seat. People turned to look, and Mrs. Jackson nodded apologies. And finally people smiled and said to one another, "Isn't it nice? That little black boy is getting culture." Pretty soon it was all over.

Except that the symphony was going on, and the man was still standing there, holding up the cymbals. Then I saw the man with the stick (I found out later he was the conductor) raise his arm toward the man with the cymbals. He moved them apart, and as the conductor's arm came down, the man holding the cymbals clapped them together. Once, twice, three times. He didn't just tap them or tinkle them. He put his whole body into the action as he crashed them together. And it was a majestic sound. One little man made a noise so grand that it could be heard above the whole symphony.

I could hardly stand it. I thought I'd burst. My arm was still in Mrs. Jackson's grip, so I leaned over and said, "Psst—I like culture. I like the symphony. I love the cymbals. I think heaven must be like this." And she said softly, "Praise the Lord." And she put her arms around me and hugged me, and I disappeared again until she let me loose.

I never forgot the symphony or the man with the cymbals. He has an important message I carry with me to this day. God gives us all something to do in life's symphony. Whatever you've been given to do, do it. But don't just do it anytime, not just when you want to, like a warm-up time, not just when some ghetto kid getting culture gets impatient and shouts, "Hit 'em!" Wait for the conductor. Do it when the conductor says do it. Then it fits the symphony.

And when you do it, don't dabble around with it. Don't tap it gently. Don't tinkle it timidly. Do it with all the strength and energy you've got to give.

Listen again, and remember the man with the cymbals.

> Praise the Lord!
> Praise God in his sanctuary;
>   praise him in his mighty firmament!
> Praise him for his mighty deeds;
>   praise him according to his surpassing greatness!
> Praise him with trumpet sound;
>   praise him with lute and harp!
> Praise him with tambourine and dance;
>   praise him with strings and pipe!
> Praise him with clanging cymbals;
>   praise him with loud clashing cymbals!
> Let everything that breathes praise the Lord.
>   PRAISE THE LORD!

31

The Year Easter Got Lost

Mark 16:1-7

John Fisher looked out his window. His spirits were as gloomy as the rainy morning, and his grumbling was augmented by the occasional rumble of the season's first thunder. He had made wonderful plans for the day.

You see, John had a green thumb. His little patch of grass and his fence-row flowers were the talk of the neighborhood. That was other years. This year, cold weather and unseasonable snow, and now this rainstorm, had kept him from even turning up the ground. It would be the first year in many that his yard work was not complete by Easter.

"If you're looking for something to do, you can wash the ceilings upstairs." John grimaced. Wasn't that just like a wife? He had a notion to tell her the job was over his head, but he was too disgruntled to even attempt a joke. Besides, Margaret had quit laughing at them years ago.

Armed with two buckets, two sponges, and his trusty box of cleanser, he made his way to the spare bedroom. A second trip provided transportation for the stepladder and he was ready to go.

As he moved the chest of drawers away from the wall, he noticed a Bible always kept in the guest room. Partly because it was the day before Easter, mostly because he wasn't anxious to clean, John picked up the Bible. He leafed to the Gospel of Mark and began reading in the sixteenth chapter.

> When the Sabbath was over, Mary Magdalene, and Mary
> the mother of James, and Salome, brought spices, so that
> they might go and anoint him. And very early on the first
> day of the week, when the sun had risen, they went to
> the tomb.

John looked up from the Scripture. It was an old story,
so familiar that he could almost complete it from memory.
But he looked down and continued reading.

> They had been saying to one another, "Who will roll
> away the stone for us from the entrance to the tomb?"
> When they looked up, they saw that the stone, which was
> very large, had already been rolled back. As they enter-
> ing the tomb, they saw a young man, dressed in a white
> robe, sitting on the right side; and they were alarmed.
> But he said to them, "Do not be alarmed; you are look-
> ing for Jesus of Nazareth, who was crucified. There he is.
> Bestow your spices and be gone!"

John bolted upright! His eyes jumped back over the passage: "You are looking for Jesus of Nazareth, who was crucified. There he is."

He hadn't read wrong. That's what it said. He read the
last few verses:

> Bestow your spices and be gone! And with heavy hearts
> the women anointed the body of Christ, and fled from
> the tomb, for they were frightened and overcome with
> bitterness and sorrow.

John Fisher sat paralyzed. He wanted to shout something,
but the cry died in his throat. Then abruptly, like one in a
nightmare, he fumbled back through the Gospel of Matthew.
His eyes raced through the chapter twenty-eight to the last
few verses. There it was again. "Go quickly, and tell his disciples that he is dead and they will see him no more."

This time his voice worked. He shouted, "Margaret!
MARGARET!" No answer. She must be in the basement.

Quickly, he leafed through Luke and John. In both cases, the account stated that the tomb was full. Then John Fisher noticed something that made his scalp tingle. The Bible ended with the Gospel of John. No Acts of the Apostles, no Pauline letters to young churches, no book of Revelation.

Margaret's voice interrupted him. "Did you call dear? Are you hurt?"

He leaped up and started for the door. He didn't even recognize his own voice. "Margaret," he shouted. "Easter is lost!"

"What do you mean, Easter is lost?" she answered from the bottom of the stairs. Then she saw John coming unsteadily down the steps. Her faced changed. "John, you're white as a sheet. What's wrong?"

"Here!" he said, thrusting the Bible at her. His trembling hands made the pages rattle. "Read this!" he fairly shouted at her. "Don't ask questions—just read it." And he sat down on the stairs. His legs wouldn't hold him any longer.

Margaret Fisher read the verses while John Fisher waited. He leaned forward as she came to the angel's words. "Do not be amazed. You are looking for Jesus of Nazareth, who was crucified. There he is! Bestow your spices. . . ."

She stopped. That can't be. The tomb was empty. She looked at John, then quickly she turned the pages as he had, reading rapidly the closing verses of the remaining gospels. She shut the Bible and for a second she looked silently at her husband. Then abruptly she turned on her heel and ran to the living room.

John, sensing her intention, jumped from the stairway and raced her to the bookcase. Margaret snatched the family Bible from its place. Her hands, suddenly all thumbs, fumbled through the thin pages and then came to rest again in the sixteenth chapter of Mark. Her trembling finger followed along the verses. It stopped unsteadily beneath the words, "Bestow your spices and be gone! And with heavy hearts the women anointed the body of Christ, and fled from the tomb. . . ."

John Fisher sat on the footstool and looked at his wife, huddled on the floor with open Bible, an expression of utter disbelief on her face. He knew that his own countenance mirrored her confusion and fear. It was impossible for this kind of thing to happen. You might easily lose the spirit of Easter in the frills of the season, but you didn't lose the actual story. The printed record just didn't cease to be.

"John," Margaret stirred. "John, let's call James."

• • •

James Fisher, age twenty-three and married eighteen wonderful months, groaned loudly at the ring of the phone. "Go away," he muttered.

Even as he did he knew it wouldn't. He could let the answering machine pick up. Still, a newspaper reporter ought not to pass up the chance to answer the phone. You never knew who might be calling. He stumbled out of bed, looking at the dismal morning, and resolved to return to his mattress as soon as the caller was dismissed,

"Hello."

"James!" He recognized his mother's voice. And he was a little irritated to hear it.

"Mom, do you realize what time it is? Call me again in about ninety minutes and I'll. . . ."

"James, Please. . . ."

The tone of her voice stopped him and he was instantly awake. "What's the matter? Is something wrong with Dad? He didn't have another. . . ."

"No son. But—well, I don't know how to explain it over the phone. Could you come over, please, right away? If Nancy's awake, bring her."

There was a pause and then she added, "And James, bring along the copy of the Bible."

"Okay Mom, I'll be right. . . . Bring along a copy of what?"

"A copy of the Bible," she answered. "A copy of the good old-fashioned, dependable Bible."

Her voice broke. "Hurry son," she said. And she hung up.

James Fisher pinched his arm. It was a habit he had of making sure he was awake. Of all the screwy ways to begin a Saturday morning, this took the cake.

"Are you awake, Nan?"

She laughed. "I have been. You were so gallant to answer the phone, to spare your lady fair the trouble." She laughed again. "What was it?"

James came back in the room. "Something's wrong over at the house. They want us to come over right away. Let's get dressed."

● ● ●

James turned the same doorknob that he could remember reaching up to open years ago. Nancy went in, and as he followed, his mother rushed into his arms. She was trembling uncontrollably. He looked across the kitchen at the ashen, constricted face of his dad. "What's the matter? You two act like the bottom just fell out!"

"It did, son. I'm afraid it did."

He led the way into the living room. He didn't know where to begin. You don't look a son in the eye and say, "All we ever believed is shot." You don't just blurt out, Easter is lost! He decided to let James read it for himself. With a small glimmer of hope that whatever his plague was, it had not affected Jimmy's Bible, he said, "Open your Bible, son, to the sixteenth chapter of Mark, and read it out loud."

"Look Dad, tomorrow's Easter Sunday. We can read the Bible then. Let me in on the problem before I read the cure."

"Read it, James, out loud, so your father and I can hear it." His mother's pleading eyes set him busy looking for Mark.

He began to read aloud the familiar story. As he came to the angel's words, John and Margaret leaned forward broadcasting the hope that fought despair in their hearts. "Do not be amazed. You are looking for Jesus of Nazareth, who was crucified. There he is. Bestow your spices and be gone!"

James Fisher stopped. Nancy spoke sharply.

"Don't be sacrilegious, Jimmy. Do what you mother and dad ask you to do. This is no time for jokes."

She watched his eyes as they jumped back to reread the words. Then she saw him look suddenly at his father. The two faces, which before had looked so different, now looked frighteningly alike. James jumped up from the chair and started for the bookcase. His father's voice stopped him in the middle of the room.

"We've already checked all our copies. They're all the same as yours. Easter seems to be lost."

• • •

Red Zager mashed his cigarette into the already stuffed ashtray. Another hour and he'd be heading home for a well earned rest. Night work on the city desk no longer held any glamour, but it was his livelihood. He leaned back. Two glorious days! He'd sleep today and maybe make it to church tomorrow, but mostly, he'd just loaf.

The phone jarred him out of his pleasant reverie. "City Desk," he barked.

"Red, this is Jimmy. Listen carefully!"

"Sure, kid, you sound like you got something hot. Go ahead!" He listened. Once he interrupted to ask a question:

"You sure you didn't have a couple too many last night that carried over into this morning?" The shout through the phone hurt his ear.

Red threw the phone back on the hook and headed for the Religion Editor's desk, all in one motion. There'd be a Bible there somewhere. In exactly four minutes, he was back and on the phone to New York. Crazy or not, the world had to know what was happening on this Saturday, the day before Easter.

• • •

The Reverend Elwood Mason paced the floor in his study. He frowned. Eight years in the ministry, and each year he had the same problem at Easter—how to capture the heart of Easter in a fresh and inspiring way.

All during the week his meditations had lifted this concern before God. He knew that around the world, pastors were facing the same concern.

He remembered with a wry smile his first Easter sermon. What a great joy it had been as he had pored through the good news of the resurrection, preparing for his message. He remembered what a thrill it had been to share in simple terms the meaning of the empty tomb. But he remembered also the comment of good old sister Miriam as she shook his hand at the door.

"Fine message, Pastor." And she patted his hand. "It's always good to have the same thing once a year."

He frowned now as he remembered the sudden jolt it gave him to realize that his best effort to make the resurrection fresh and meaningful had been passed off as the same old thing.

He looked at the notes for his unfinished sermon, scattered across the desk. It was the same old thing. He sat down and he put his head in his hands.

"O God," he prayed. "Why does the miracle of this most special day becomes so commonplace? Why is it that so great a message becomes old hat? For your namesake, O Lord, give me words to help make this a season of newfound joy."

The phone brought his prayer to an abrupt end. It was John Fisher and he sounded distraught.

• • •

It was ten o'clock Saturday evening, the year that Easter got lost. The Reverend Mason still paced the floor, but this time he was wearing out the carpet in his living room. His wife was in the kitchen filling Easter baskets. Let the roof fall in on the Christian faith, but mothers still care for the happiness of little ones.

What a terrible day it had been. What had begun as a rainy Saturday before Easter had turned out to be nightmarish in every way. And what had been a small but earnest prayer for something new to say had become a daylong intercession for words, any words.

Not a single account of the empty tomb could be found anywhere in the city—or anywhere in the world, according to news reports. How could he say, "Remember the empty tomb? Remember how it used to be, before all the accounts got lost?"

His first reaction had been to give a prophetic, serves you right sermon, upbraiding the people for taking the Easter message for granted all these years. But he thought of the people, how their confusion was as great as his, and he rejected the idea.

He switched on the TV with a kind of hopeless notion that somewhere around the world the good news of the empty grave might have been found. He watched the beer commercial, "It doesn't get any better than this," and then listened intently as his favorite newscaster began.

"Good evening, ladies and gentlemen, or can I really say *good*? Today will go down in history as the day that Easter got lost.

"It is still a mystery to all concerned how every account of the resurrection of Jesus Christ has been stricken from all written accounts and from all sacred music. Informed sources say that a worldwide search for just one copy of the printed account is still in progress. Here in the United States, both political parties have offered rewards for originals.

"The National Association of Evangelicals has issued a statement saying, 'It serves the world right.' The National Council of Churches has been in executive session since nine A.M. An unofficial spokesman for the group indicated its members were as puzzled as everyone else.

"In Rome, the Pope has called an emergency meeting of the College of Cardinals. As yet he has refused to make any official statement. However, he is expected to speak at any moment to the huge throng of over two hundred thousand gathered in St. Peter's Square.

"In Virginia, Pat Robertson has agreed to fly his jet anywhere in the world, free of charge, to pick up any preserved copy. According to unidentified sources at the Christian Broadcasting Network, Robertson has commented privately that this may indeed be the beginning of Armageddon."

The announcer continued his rapid fire delivery.

"An official spokesman for the Pentagon said that in the light of the disappearance of the resurrection and the promise of eternal life, top brass are reconsidering the seriousness of nuclear proliferation. A state department aide, in an afternoon press conference, said that he is confident the U.S. is ahead of the Cubans, the Iraqis, and the Chinese in the search for an original document.

"In major cities across our nation, clergy and Christians, or whatever we can call then now, have spent a confusing day preparing for tomorrow. The mayor of New York says the traditional Easter Day Parade will go on as scheduled on Fifth Avenue. But beneath the surface of this gaiety will ride a sense of foreboding and gloom, as those who have regularly shown off their bonnets will this year, literally, have nothing on which to hang their hats."

Reverend Mason pushed the remote control just as the beer commercial began the second time. He felt sick to his stomach. And tomorrow—tomorrow was the day to give something to a people who found, just today, that they had nothing.

• • •

On the following morning, the church was full. The custodian was busy setting up chairs in the basement, to accommodate the overflow crowd.

Reverend Mason followed the choir in during the prelude. He looked at the sea of faces. The bright clothes, impossible hats, and beautiful flowers constrasted sharply with the empty, haunted look that he saw in their eyes. He thought bitterly of yesterday when he had wanted something new to say. He patted the notes of his original sermon, which, from force of habit he had put in the usual pocket. It was really old stuff now. It wasn't any good for today.

On impulse, he departed from the usual order of worship and walked to the pulpit Bible. As he turned the pages, he could hear the silent screaming in the hearts of the five hundred people before him. May as well read it and get it over with.

He began a careful and measured reading of the first five verses. And then, with a mixture of hope and fear, he read verses five and six:

As they entering the tomb, they saw a young man, dressed in a white robe, sitting on the right side; and they were alarmed. But he said to them, "Do not be alarmed; you are looking for Jesus of Nazareth, who was crucified. He has been raised; he is not here. Look, there is the place they lad him.

The Reverend Mason stopped short in disbelief. The congregation began to buzz in a threatening roar.

"Wait," he shouted, and he read it again. "It's true! It's true!"

He pounded on the Bible, a thing he never did. "It's right here where it always was before yesterday! It is the same as it has always been."

Quickly he took out his notes from his pocket and began to tell the joyous news of the empty tomb. And the people listened—people like John and Margaret Fisher, James and Nan, and Red Zager.

It was the best news they had heard for many a day.

• • •

Somewhere, where time is not measured and things are not as they are here, the Lord God looked down and saw the events in Reverend Elwood Mason's church duplicated thousands of times in churches all around the world. The Lord God listened to the inspired preaching of the servants of the Word and watched the eager listening of all the people.

The Almighty smiled. While it was not customary to intervene in human affairs, this time God couldn't resist the combined prayers of 856,921 clergy who prayed for an Easter message that would be welcomed as joyful good news.

God put a date in the book, and marked beside it, "The Year Easter Got Lost." Under "Comments," the great hand paused, then wrote, "Second-best Easter the world has ever had."

32

A Conversation with God

1 Sam. 3:1-20

This sermon was delivered January 20, 1991, the Sunday after the start of the Persian Gulf War. The setting included a table, a chair, and a telephone set in the middle of the open chancel. The sermon was delivered from a sitting position, as a telephone monologue (much in the style of Bob Newhart's phone monologues) with the phone held to the ear, and short periods of "listening"—silence as the conversation took place.

It's unusual for me to speak from this position. Events of the past week have created all kinds of emotions for us.

Thursday morning I was sitting here in my office trying to decide what I should do. My sermon titled, "Somebody Special" was already finished. Using the reading for the day from 1 Samuel 3, I tried to work around such questions as, Does God still speak to us in this day? and if so, Do we have to be somebody special to hear God's voice? Or does God speak and we aren't in a position to hear or recognize what we hear as the voice of God?

I had just said to myself, "Lord if you still do speak, then make it plain what I should be doing this Sunday morning. Should I change my sermon?" Then the phone rang. This is what happened.

Hello! Yes, this is Earle Fike.

What do you mean, "What do I want?" You called me. I didn't call you.

Who is this ?

The Lord of all? God? Yeah, sure. Who is this really? If you're trying to sell something, I don't buy things over the phone.

Yes, I did call for help. Yes, I am trying to decide what to do. Yes, last night I did dream about. . . . How did you know that?

Yes, sir—or yes, ma'am. I can't tell which it is by your voice.

Oh, that's the way it's supposed to be. Okay.

Yes, I would be glad to have a conversation with you. Yes—yes, I know that Samuel said, "Speak, for your servant is listening."

Absolutely—yes. Oh! I am to do mostly listening? Okay.

May I ask questions? All right. But I am to repeat out loud the answers you give so you know I'm getting the message.

What initiated this call? Well, it's this way Lord. We started a war again. We can't seem to figure out how to get along without them. There's all this material in the New Testament from Jesus about non-violence and love. There's a lot about how to deal with conflict without killing off our brothers and sisters—things like going the second mile and turning the other cheek, treating others with love like we'd like to be treated. But we can't seem to put those things to-gether with the way we live with one another. We excuse our behavior by saying ,"It's only human to fight," and we quote your Word by saying that you warned us there would be wars and rumors of wars. So, here we go again. Talking about how we didn't want to do it, but it was absolutely necessary.

Yeah, I do feel bad about it. Well actually, worse than that. I feel sad and disappointed and ashamed. I feel terrible. And

I think a lot of people do. And the problem is, I have people coming to church Sunday morning and I don't know what to say to them about all of this.

What sort of things do I feel? Well, I don't think it's the time to point fingers and say who's to blame.

Okay, we agree. Yes, I do remember that's your job, and you'll take care of all the necessary judging. And I do remember that we will all come under that judgment—whether we made big decisions to actually attack or whether we made little decisions about lifestyle that helped to create the crisis.

Could I ask a question? I don't believe in war. I don't like war. I think it's evil and not your way. But how am I to respond now that it's in process? I get caught up in winning. I want it to be over. Can I pray for a quick victory? If I do, isn't that supporting the war? See, I don't want thousands of people to die. I want it to be over as soon as possible. Am I betraying my convictions if I pray for it to be over quickly?

I understand. Any prayers that are said out of compassion for those who lose their lives, or those who suffer, or those who wait fearfully for loved ones are important. More than important—they are required.

Yes, I remember that such prayers are to be for friend and enemy. Yes, I do remember that what we do for the least and the lost we do to you.

There's more? I see. It's not too late for that? We are also to pray for the leaders of the nations, that they may find ways to reduce and stop the bloodshed and violence. You of course mean Saddam Hussein.

Oh! Saddam and all the rest of us. Yes, you're right. Those are things we can all do.

But what about this, Lord? I heard a university student who was protesting a peace rally say, "To seek a new world order for peace you need to back it with force. There is no other way." Lord, if the war is over quickly and the win is decisive, won't that prove his point? We won't have learned anything other than that violence works, will we?

I am to say carefully what I hear. Okay. I am to help the people remember that we thought if we sent thousands of our troops over there with thousands of pieces of military hardware, that when Saddam saw our power he would come to his senses and leave.

No, you're right, that power didn't work.

I am to help the people remember that we thought if we had a worldwide alliance that set a deadline for Saddam to be out of Kuwait or the use of armed force would be acceptable, that he would get the message and retreat.

No, you're right—that didn't work either.

I am to help the people remember that the President felt if Congress gave him the authority to begin war after January fifteenth, and we made clear we would go to war if he didn't vacate Kuwait, that Saddam would finally get the message and leave. And that didn't work either. And you count all these shows of force as a failure?

I see. I hadn't thought of it that way. It's hard to speak about peaceful ways to settle difference while threatened.

I am to remind the people that after World War II, there were those who were saying that we should attack Russia right away, because even though we fought with them against Germany, they were really not to be trusted. I didn't know that—I guess I was too young.

You mean there were those who said we should do it now while they were weak—we should wipe them out now so that we wouldn't have to fight them later? You mean there were actually those who were arguing it would save lives of persons if we did it quickly? But Lord, we didn't do it. Why?

I see. Some people do hear your voice and recognize it. You speak through voices that say war is not the right way; and there were some strong voices who were heard.

Yes—now that you mention it, I agree. It took us over forty years to work out our relationship with Russia, but it does seem to me to be better than wiping them out earlier. But let's be honest, Lord. Do you think anyone will buy that example of not using force? Oh, I'm to say it anyway? Okay.

Yes, I'm still listening. I am to remind the people that there are examples of use of power that are less violent than war, that you speak through the words and actions of people who live in and deal creatively with conflict situations.

Yes, I'm sure everyone has heard of Gandhi. But he was special. Not many like him come along. And besides, there were people who lost their lives, God. The overthrow of the English rule in India could hardly be called non-violent.

Oh, I see. There is a difference between being willing to be killed for your convictions and in being willing to kill for them. Oh—that's the major difference.

Okay, I'll say that. Yes, of course, I remember the cross— I think most of us do. But I don't think we think that example applies to us. After all, we're not your Son.

Ah—yes. Okay, I accept that. We're your children and that's what being an example means. I'll remind the people.

I'm—I'm still listening and repeating. What would happen if Saddam tried Gandhi's power? That's too much of a stretch, Lord; I can't even imagine it. He's a madman.

You say I should be thankful he doesn't understand that it's a way he could actually win? How is that? I am to ask the people, what if he loaded up all his artillery, all his weapons, and said to the Allied forces: "We will not fight anymore. I'm bringing all weapons to the border to give them up. The Iraqi armies are disarmed, but under Allah, we believe our cause is just. We will not fight you, but Kuwait is a part of us and we will not leave. You must kill us all—unarmed men, women, and children, if you want us out, but we will not go home because we are already home."

What if he said that? Well, he won't! And you know his cause isn't just.

Oh, that's not the issue. It's just an example and the question is, What would our kind of power do in the face of that kind of power? I don't know. That's not a kind of power we know very much about.

Yes—I see. I know all about using examples. I try to do that every Sunday.

Yes, I see the connection. There is a difference in being willing to die for what you believe and in being willing to kill for what you believe. But if you don't mind me saying so—Lord—you aren't making it any easier.

But I'm still in trouble, Lord. What will I say, to all who say that going to war is the human way? What will I say to all those who say you said, "There will be wars and rumors of wars," and we're not going to change human nature?

Yes, I'm listening carefully. I am to remind them that until some four hundred years ago, about the time of Shakespeare, there had always been human sacrifice somewhere on the earth. And I am to remind them that until the nineteenth century, dueling was an accepted way to settle differences between persons. Yes, I remember the story about Alexander Hamilton. And I am to remind them that until the Emancipation Proclamation in 1863, slavery was acceptable in this country.

Yes, I agree that these things have pretty much died out. You're right—human nature hasn't changed, but it has come under some control. I will say that.

But what . . . Okay. You're not finished yet. I'm listening.

For that reason, you think we may be making progress and you haven't given up hope? Yes, I hope this too. I hope we're learning that either war is finished or we are.

What? You mean there is something in this war that we can point to as promising? I could use a little good news.

You're pleased there is less joy over this war than other recent ones? You're pleased that there is more sadness than joy, more quiet seriousness than raucous celebrating? You are pleased that not many people are talking about kicking butt and enjoying it. You are pleased that there is more of a sense of failure that we weren't able to avoid war.

Yes, I've noticed all that, but I didn't interpret it as some sign of hope. Maybe we're learning something about the foolishness of war. That's a good sign—I'll take heart in it.

No, I didn't see that on television. What happened?

I am to remind people about the reporter who spoke to the wife of a serviceman overseas. She was holding their child. Hoping to get patriotic support from her, he said, "The word is that the war is going well and there may be a great victory. How does that make you feel?" Speaking right out of your heart, she looked directly into the camera and told millions of people, "Going to war is never a victory."

I wish I had seen that. Yes, I do believe that you speak through the words of everyday people.

That reminds me, Lord: what can be said to all of us who feel helpless, who have convictions about war but don't see anything for one person to do? You'll give me a list. Right.

- You say we can pray for all involved and for a swift end to the hostilities. I think millions of people are already doing that. Okay, I'll tell the people not to quit.

- You say we can refuse to be seduced by power, refuse to be fooled by success into believing that going to war is a good way to settle differences. That may be harder for us, Lord. I don't know whether we have the tenacity or the energy.

- Oh, I should use the word *energy* with care. Before you land on me for that issue, you know very well that I've often said I would rather pay three dollars a gallon for gas than to go over there and kill people to keep the price at $1.10. But you say that's not the issue—the issue is lifestyle. You say that each of us can make an individual commitment to use less energy so that we aren't backed into a corner and have to fight. God, do you think that would really influence national priorities? I see. You're saying if enough people believed it, it would have an effect, but whether it would or not, at least as individuals we would be faithful.

- You want me to remind people that in everyday situations of conflict; we can begin to practice understanding and negotiation—not wimpish submission, but caring confrontation. Okay, I'll remind them.

- And finally, you're going to give me a quote to put on my desk for the duration of the war? Okay. What is it? It's by Adlai Stevenson! I thought it would be some Scripture verse. Yes, I remember that you speak through everyday people. The quote is: "We do not hold the vision of a world without conflict. We do hold the vision of a world without war—and this inevitably requires an alternative system for coping with conflict." I like it— I'll put it on my desk.

Do I have other questions? Oh yes, hundreds on other subjects, but I want to think a while on this conversation.

You know, Lord, this isn't anywhere close to the way you spoke to Samuel.

Oh. I guess that's right. Having a conversation with you is pretty close to what went on.

Yes, I will remember that God speaks to people if they listen. And, yes, I would like to do this again sometime. I'll really look forward to it.

It was —well, different. Thanks. And goodbye.

Oh, with you it's never goodbye—you're always with us. So what should I say? Okay—I'll see you later.

The Author

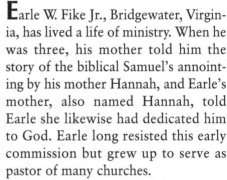

Earle W. Fike Jr., Bridgewater, Virginia, has lived a life of ministry. When he was three, his mother told him the story of the biblical Samuel's annointing by his mother Hannah, and Earle's mother, also named Hannah, told Earle she likewise had dedicated him to God. Earle long resisted this early commission but grew up to serve as pastor of many churches.

Fike's first assignment, in 1954, was at Meyersdale (Pa.) Church of the Brethren (COB). He went on to pastor three more congregations in Chicago and Pennsylvania in a rich variety of cultural settings, from inner city Chicago through the "rural going toward urban" college town setting of Elizabethtown, Pennsylvania.

A past moderator of the COB, he has been a staff member at the COB General Board in Elgin, Illinois and has been a member of the Bethany Theological Seminary faculty. He chaired the committee that produced the COB manual *For All Who Minister* and was for ten years on the board of Bethany Seminary Board of Trustees, which he chaired for three years. He has had published two books, including *Please Pray With Me* (Brethren Press, 1990) and many articles.

Earle and Jean Kiser Fike have been married fifty years and have a daughter, two sons, and five granchildren. They are members of the Bridgewater Church of the Brethren.